The Complete Beginner's Guide to Learning Greek

Learn Basic Conversational Phrases,
Real-life Vocabulary, Proper Grammar,
and Pronunciation in 15–20 Minutes a
Day

M. J. Perreault

Contents

Introduction   VI

Chapter 1: Foundations of Greek   1

   1.1 The Greek Alphabet: A Comprehensive Guide

   1.2 Vowel and Consonant Sounds

   1.3 Phonetic Pronunciation Basics

   1.4 Common Greetings and Introductions

   1.5 Numbers and Basic Counting

   1.6 Days of the Week and Months of the Year

Chapter 2: Essential Grammar Basics   18

   2.1 Subject Pronouns and Basic Sentence Structure

   2.2 Present Tense Verb Conjugations

   2.3 Definite and Indefinite Articles

   2.4 Basic Noun Cases and Their Uses

   2.5 Adjectives and Agreement

   2.6 Questions and Negations

Chapter 3: Daily Life Vocabulary   33

   3.1 Food and Dining Vocabulary

   3.2 Shopping and Market Vocabulary

   3.3 Directions and Transportation

   3.4 Travel and Accommodation Phrases

3.5 Health and Emergency Vocabulary

3.6 Weather and Seasons

Chapter 4: Conversational Phrases   48

4.1 Introducing Yourself and Others

4.2 Asking for Help and Information

4.3 Making Small Talk

4.4 Expressing Preferences and Opinions

4.5 Talking About Daily Activities

4.6 Making Plans and Arrangements

Review Page   61

Chapter 5: Pronunciation and Listening Practice   63

5.1 Common Pronunciation Mistakes and How to Avoid
Them

5.2 Listening to Native Speakers

5.3 Mimicking Native Pronunciation

5.4 Phonetic Transcription Exercises

5.5 Tongue Twisters for Pronunciation Practice

5.6 Using Audio Resources Effectively

Chapter 6: Cultural Context and Insights   75

6.1 Greek Customs and Traditions

6.2 Cultural Etiquette and Social Norms

6.3 Important Greek Holidays and Festivals

6.4 Greek Cuisine and Dining Etiquette

6.5 Greek Mythology and Its Influence on Language

6.6 Contemporary Greek Society

Chapter 7: Interactive Exercises and Practice   89

7.1 Fill-in-the-Blank Grammar Exercises

7.2 Vocabulary Matching Games

7.3 Dialogue Practice Scenarios

7.4 Self-Assessment Quizzes

7.5 Role-Playing Exercises

7.6 Writing Practice: Simple Sentences and Paragraphs

Chapter 8: Advanced Beginner Topics   103

8.1 Past Tense Verb Conjugations

8.2 Future Tense Basics

8.3 Compound Sentences and Conjunctions

8.4 Introduction to Reflexive Verbs

8.5 Indirect and Direct Object Pronouns

8.6 Common Idiomatic Expressions

Conclusion   117

References   120

Introduction

This book is designed to help you avoid those early struggles and set you on a smooth path to learning Greek. Its purpose is to provide a comprehensive yet beginner-friendly guide to mastering basic conversational phrases, real-life vocabulary, proper grammar, and pronunciation. Think of it as your companion on this exciting journey.

You'll find practical tools in these pages to help you speak Greek quickly. We start with basic conversational phrases for greetings, introductions, and everyday interactions. This will help you start speaking right away. Then, we move on to vocabulary relevant to daily life, like food, travel, shopping, and directions. You'll also find clear explanations of grammar basics, including verb conjugation, noun cases, and sentence structure. Each section comes with examples to aid your understanding. Pronunciation guides, cultural notes, and exercises are also included to reinforce your learning.

Why learn Greek? For starters, it enhances your travel experiences. Imagine exploring the beautiful islands of Greece, chatting with locals, and understanding the rich history and culture of the region. Learning Greek also broadens your linguistic skills and opens doors to new friendships and opportunities. Whether you have Greek heritage or a profound interest in Greek culture, this language connects you to a rich and ancient world.

This book is for beginners. Whether you're learning Greek for travel, cultural interest, a connection to heritage, or educational purposes, you'll find the tools you need here. The book's unique features are designed to make your learning experience enjoyable and effective. Phonetic pronunciation guides help you say words correctly. Practical vocabulary ensures you learn words you'll use. Audio resources allow you to hear and practice the language. Cultural insights give you a more profound understanding of how language reflects Greek customs. The step-by-step progression ensures you build a solid foundation before moving on to more advanced topics.

I know that learning a new language can be daunting. But I want to assure you that you can do it with consistent effort and the right resources. This book is designed to be your guide and support system. Take it one step at a time, and don't be afraid to make mistakes. Every error is a learning opportunity. Celebrate your progress, no matter how small. Remember, every incredible journey begins with a single step.

So, let's get started. Open the first chapter and begin your journey to learning Greek. With each page, you'll gain new skills and confidence. You're not alone in this; I'm here to guide you every step of the way. Let's make this journey enjoyable and rewarding. Welcome to the adventure of learning Greek!

Chapter 1: Foundations of Greek

H ave you ever tried to read a street sign in a foreign country and felt utterly lost? I remember standing in the middle of Athens, staring at a street sign written in Greek, and feeling utterly confused. The letters looked familiar yet different, and I couldn't make sense of the words. It was then that I realized the importance of learning the Greek alphabet. Understanding the alphabet is the first step to unlocking the language. It opens the door to reading, writing, and pronouncing Greek words correctly.

1.1 The Greek Alphabet: A Comprehensive Guide

The Greek alphabet is the cornerstone of the Greek language. It consists of 24 letters, each with an uppercase and a lowercase form. Unlike the Latin alphabet, which you're more familiar with, the Greek alphabet includes several unique letters. Let's start by looking at the alphabet chart:

Alphabet Chart

Uppercase: Α, Β, Γ, Δ, Ε, Ζ, Η, Θ, Ι, Κ, Λ, Μ, Ν, Ξ, Ο, Π, Ρ, Σ, Τ, Υ, Φ, Χ, Ψ, Ω

Lowercase: α, β, γ, δ, ε, ζ, η, θ, ι, κ, λ, μ, ν, ξ, ο, π, ρ, σ, τ, υ, φ, χ, ψ, ω

Each letter has a distinct pronunciation. For example, Α (alpha) sounds like the "a" in "father," while Β (beta) sounds like the "v" in "victory." Understanding these pronunciations is crucial for reading and speaking Greek effectively. The Greek alphabet was adopted from the Phoenician alphabet around the 9th–8th centuries BC. Unlike the Phoenician alphabet, which was consonant-based, the Greeks added vowels to make the language more versatile and easier to read.

To practice writing the alphabet, start with tracing exercises. This helps you get a feel for the letters' shapes. Once you're comfortable, use blank lines for freehand practice. Write each letter repeatedly, both in uppercase and lowercase, to build muscle mem-ory. For context, try writing simple words like "καλημέρα" (good morning) and "σπίτι" (house).

spiti

A fun way to memorize the alphabet is through a song. Here's a simple song to help you remember the letters:

Α, Β, Γ, Δ, Ε, Ζ, Η, Θ,

Ι, Κ, Λ, Μ, Ν, Ξ, Ο, Π,

Ρ, Σ, Τ, Υ, Φ, Χ, Ψ, Ω.

The melody is similar to the "Alphabet Song" in English. You can find an audio resource to practice this song online. Sing it a few times, and you'll find that the letters stick in your memory more efficiently. Mnemonics and repetition are also helpful. Try associating each letter with a word or image that starts with the same sound.

Comparing the Greek alphabet to the Latin alphabet can also be enlightening. For instance, the Greek letter A (alpha) is similar to the Latin letter A in appearance and sound. However, some letters, like Ψ (psi), have no direct equivalent in the Latin alphabet. This letter sounds like the "PS" in "lapse." Understanding these similarities and differences can prevent confusion and help you learn more efficiently.

Here's a visual comparison chart to highlight these points:

Visual Comparison Chart

Greek Alphabet: A, B, Γ, Δ, E, Z, H, Θ, I, K, Λ, M, N, Ξ, O, Π, P, Σ, T, Υ, Φ, X, Ψ, Ω

Latin Alphabet: A, B, C, D, E, Z, H, I, J, K, L, M, N, X, O, P, Q, R, S, T, U, V, W, Y, Z

As you can see, fundamental differences exist while there are some similarities. For example, the Greek letter H (eta) sounds like the "ee" in "see," whereas the Latin letter H has a different sound. These differences can be tricky, but with practice, you'll start to recognize and remember them.

Understanding the historical context of the Greek alphabet adds depth to your learning. It was developed during the Iron Age, centuries after the loss of Linear B, which was used for Mycenaean Greek. This adaptation allowed the Greeks to preserve their language and expand it eastwards to Phrygia and westwards to the Etruscans, influencing the Latin alphabet. Notable early inscriptions include the Dipylon inscription and Nestor's Cup from the late 8th century BC, which match Phoenician letter forms of around 800–750 BC.

Mastering the Greek alphabet lays a strong foundation for further learning. You'll find reading signs, menus, and simple texts much more straightforward. Plus, you'll be able to write your notes and practice pronunciation more effectively. Remember, the key is consistent practice. Write a few letters daily, sing the alphabet song, and compare the Greek letters with their Latin counterparts. You'll become comfortable with the Greek alphabet with time and effort, setting the stage for more advanced language skills.

1.2 Vowel and Consonant Sounds

Understanding vowel and consonant sounds is crucial for speaking and reading Greek effectively. The Greek language is syllabic, making it easier to break down words and pronounce them correctly. Let's start with vowels. Greek has seven vowels: α, ε, η, ι, ο, ω, υ. Each vowel has a unique sound. For instance, α sounds like the "a" in "apple," while ε sounds like the "e" in "egg." The vowels η, ι, and υ all sound like "ee" in "teeth," but their usage varies depending on the word. The vowels ο and ω sound like the "o" in "box," yet they are used in different contexts. Understanding these nuances will help you read and pronounce Greek words more accurately.

In Greek, vowels can be short or long. For example, the vowel α can be short, as in "πάπια" (duck), or long, as in "μάνα" (mother). The vowel length often depends on the word's stress and context. Pronunciation guides can help you get these sounds right. You can find audio clips online that demonstrate the correct pronunciation of each vowel. Listening to these clips and repeating the sounds will help you develop a natural accent.

Greek consonants include sounds that may be familiar to you and some that are unique. For instance, the letter β sounds like the "v" in "victory," and γ can be pronounced as a soft "y" or a hard "g," depending on its position in the word. Greek consonants can be categorized as hard or soft. For example, κ (kappa) is a hard consonant, while σ (sigma) is soft. Some consonants, like γ, have multiple pronunciations. When γ is followed by a front vowel (ε, η, ι), it sounds like the "y" in "yes." But when it appears before a back vowel (α, ο, ω), it sounds like the "g" in "go."

Greek also has common consonant clusters, such as μπ, ντ, and γκ. These clusters are pronounced differently than their letters. For example, μπ sounds like "b" in "boy," ντ sounds like "d" in "dog," and γκ sounds like "g" in "golf." Understanding these clusters is essential for accurate pronunciation. Practice saying words like "μπανάνα" (banana), "ντομάτα" (tomato), and "αγκαλιά" (hug) to get a feel for these sounds.

Diphthongs are combinations of two vowel sounds within the same syllable. Common Greek diphthongs include αι, ει, οι, υι, ου, αυ, ευ, and ηυ. Each diphthong has a distinct sound. For example, αι sounds like the "e" in "egg," while ει and οι sound like "ee" in "teeth." The diphthong ου sounds like "oo" in "school." Diphthongs αυ, and ευ can be pronounced as "af" or "av" and "ef" or "ev," respectively, depending on the following consonant. The diphthong ηυ is less common and can be pronounced as "if" or "iv."

Fill-in-the-blank exercises can be beneficial for practicing these sounds. For instance, you can practice filling in the correct vowel or consonant in words like "π_τά" (fill in "ο" to make "ποτά" - drinks) or "κ_λός" (fill in "α" to make "καλός" - good). Matching exercises can also reinforce your learning. Match sounds to their corresponding letters or clusters. Listening and repeating audio exercises will further solidify your understanding. Find recordings of native speakers and mimic their pronunciation. This method is particularly effective for mastering tricky sounds and diphthongs.

While learning these vowel and consonant sounds might seem daunting initially, consistent practice will make them second nature. Use the resources available, such as audio clips and pronunciation guides. Practice speaking and listening as much as possible. Repetition is key. The more you practice, the more natural these sounds will become, and you'll find yourself confidently pronouncing Greek words.

1.3 Phonetic Pronunciation Basics

Understanding phonetic transcriptions is a game-changer when learning Greek. It allows you to visualize the sounds of words, making pronunciation much more manageable. Phonetic transcription uses the International Phonetic Alphabet (IPA) to represent each sound. For example, the word "καλημέρα" (good morning) is transcribed as [ka.li'me.ra]. Each symbol represents a specific sound, and the apostrophe indicates stress on the syllable "μέ." Learning these symbols may seem daunting initially, but they provide a clear guide to pronouncing Greek words correctly. You can find IPA charts online to help you familiarize yourself with these symbols.

Let's look at some common words and their IPA transcriptions to put this into practice. Take "γεια" (hello), which is transcribed as [ja]. Notice how the symbol [j] represents a sound similar to the "y" in "yes." Another example is "ευχαριστώ" (thank you), which is transcribed as [ef.xa.ris'to]. Here, the [x] represents a sound like the "ch" in the German word "Bach," and the stress falls on the last syllable. Practicing these transcriptions can dramatically improve your pronunciation. Try transcribing a few simple words yourself, then compare your results with IPA guides to see how you did.

Stress and intonation are equally crucial in Greek. Unlike English, where stress can be subtle, Greek uses clear stress marks to indicate which syllable to emphasize. For instance, in "καλημέρα," the stress mark is on the second-to-last syllable: "μέ." Incorrect stress placement can change the meaning of a word, so it's crucial to get it right. For example, "πρόσβαση" (access) with stress on the first syllable is different from "προσαύξηση" (increase), which has stress on the second syllable. Practice reading aloud and paying attention to where the stress marks are placed. Over time, this will become second nature.

Intonation patterns also play a role in how sentences are understood. In questions, the pitch generally rises at the end of the sentence, similar to English. For example, "Πώς είσαι;" (How are you?) has a rising intonation at the end. Statements tend to have a more even or falling intonation. For instance, "Είμαι καλά" (I am well) maintains a steady pitch. Practicing these patterns can help you sound more natural and fluent. Listen to native speakers and mimic their intonation. This can be done through audio resources or conversations with native speakers.

Common pronunciation mistakes often trip up beginners. Mispronouncing vowels and consonants is a frequent issue. For example, the vowel η should be pronounced like "ee" in "see," but beginners often pronounce it as "i" in "sit." Consonants like γ can also be tricky. When followed by a front vowel, γ is pronounced like "y" in "yes," but when it precedes a back vowel, it sounds like "g" in "go." Incorrect stress placement is another common mistake. Misplacing stress can change the meaning of words and make your speech sound awkward. To avoid these pitfalls, practice regularly and seek feedback from native speakers.

Pronunciation drills are invaluable for reinforcing correct pronunciation. Start with a simple repetition of complex sounds. For example, practice the sound [j] by repeating words like "γιαγιά" (grandmother). Move on to sentence-level practice, focusing on intonation and stress.

Try reading sentences aloud, paying attention to the stress marks and intonation patterns. Audio resources can guide you through this process. Listen to recordings, repeat after the speaker, and record yourself to compare. This method is particularly effective for honing your pronunciation skills and ensuring you sound more natural.

By practicing these phonetic principles, you'll find that your pronunciation improves steadily. Each small step, from understanding IPA symbols to mastering intonation patterns, brings you closer to speaking Greek confidently.

1.4 Common Greetings and Introductions

Navigating social interactions in Greek started with mastering some basic greetings. Imagine walking into a bustling Greek bakery early in the morning. The warm smell of fresh bread fills the air. You want to greet the friendly baker behind the counter. In Greek, you would say, "Καλημέρα!" (Good morning). This phrase is used until noon. As the day progresses, and you find yourself enjoying a scenic sunset at a café, "Καλησπέρα!" (Good evening) becomes the appropriate greeting. To keep things simple when meeting someone at any time of day, you can use "Γειά σου" (Hello/Hi) in informal settings or "Γειά σας" for a more formal or plural context.

Introducing yourself in Greek is straightforward, but knowing the correct phrases can make a big difference. When meeting someone new, you might say, "Με λένε..." (My name is...), followed by your name. If you want to ask someone their name, you would say, "Πώς σε λένε;" in an informal setting. For a more formal approach or when addressing a group, "Πώς σας λένε;" is appropriate. These nuances are important in Greek culture, where respect and politeness are highly valued.

Understanding social etiquette in Greece can enhance your interactions. Greeks often greet each other with a handshake or a kiss on both cheeks, depending on how well they know each other. When meeting someone for the first time, a firm handshake is customary. However, friends and family members typically greet each other with a kiss on each cheek. The use of formal and informal addresses is also significant. "Γειά σας" is used in formal situations or when addressing someone older or in a position of authority, while "Γειά σου" is reserved for friends, family, and peers. Common polite expressions include "Ευχαριστώ" (Thank you) and "Παρακαλώ" (You're welcome), which are essential in everyday interactions.

To put these greetings and introductions into practice, let's look at some sample dialogues. Imagine you're meeting a colleague for the first time:

Dialogue Example:

- Person A: Καλημέρα! Με λένε Μαρία. (Good morning! My name is Maria.)

- Person B: Καλημέρα, Μαρία. Πώς σας λένε; (Good morning, Maria. What is your name?)

- Person A: Με λένε Γιώργος. Χαίρω πολύ. (My name is George. Nice to meet you.)

- Person B: Χαίρω πολύ, Γιώργος. (Nice to meet you, George.)

Practicing these dialogues can help you feel more comfortable during real-life interactions. Role-playing exercises are an excellent way to reinforce your learning. Pair up with a friend or practice in front of a mirror. Try filling in the blanks in dialogues to test your understanding. For instance:

Fill-in-the-Blank Exercise:

- Person A: Καλησπέρα! _____ Μαρία. (Good evening!
  My name is Maria.)

- Person B: Καλησπέρα, Μαρία. Πώς _____; (Good
  evening, Maria. What is your name?)

- Person A: Με λένε Γιώργος. _____ πολύ. (My name is
  George. Nice to meet you.)

- Person B: Χαίρω πολύ, _____. (Nice to meet you,
  George.)

To further enhance your practice, listen to audio resources that
provide examples of native speakers using these phrases. Repeating
after the audio can improve your pronunciation and intonation. This
method is beneficial for getting the nuances of stress and rhythm in
Greek speech.

Understanding these basic greetings and introductions, along with
their cultural context, will make your interactions in Greek more natural and enjoyable. Whether you are greeting a vendor at a local market
or introducing yourself to a new friend, these phrases will help you
confidently navigate social situations.

1.5 Numbers and Basic Counting

When I started learning Greek, numbers seemed like a daunting hur-
dle. Yet, once I grasped the basics, I found that numbers opened up
a new world of practical applications. Greek numbers are integral to
everyday life, from telling time to shopping at the local market. Let's
start with cardinal numbers, the basic numbers used for counting.

Cardinal Numbers

The Greek numbers from 1 to 100 are as follows:

1: ένα (ena)

2: δύο (dyo)

3: τρία (tria)

4: τέσσερα (tessera)

5: πέντε (pente)

6: έξι (eksi)

7: επτά (epta)

8: οκτώ (okto)

9: εννέα (ennea)

10: δέκα (deka)

20: είκοσι (eikosi)

30: τριάντα (trianta)

40: σαράντα (saranta)

50: πενήντα (peninta)

60: εξήντα (eksinta)

70: εβδομήντα (evdominta)

80: ογδόντα (ogdonta)

90: ενενήντα (eneninta)

100: εκατό (ekato)

These numbers form the building blocks for more significant numbers. For example, 25 is είκοσι πέντε (eikosi pente), and 68 is εξήντα οκτώ (eksinta okto). Understanding these basics allows you to construct any number. To help you practice, listen to audio clips of native speakers pronouncing these numbers. Repeating after the audio can cement these sounds in your mind.

Numbers in context can be efficient. Imagine you're at a Greek market and must ask for five apples. You
would say, "Πέντε μήλα, παρακαλώ"
(Pente mila, parakalo). Or perhaps
you need to give your phone number:
"Το τηλέφωνό μου είναι δύο, ένα, τρία,

Pente mila

τέσσερα, πέντε, έξι" (To tilefono mou
einai dyo, ena, tria, tessera, pente, eksi). Practicing these numbers in
real-world scenarios can make your learning more effective.

Ordinal Numbers

Ordinal numbers indicate the position or order of things. Here are
the Greek ordinal numbers from first to tenth:

First: πρώτος (protos)

Second: δεύτερος (defteros)

Third: τρίτος (tritos)

Fourth: τέταρτος (tetartos)

Fifth: πέμπτος (pemptos)

Sixth: έκτος (ektos)

Seventh: έβδομος (evdomos)

Eighth: όγδοος (ogdoos)

Ninth: ένατος (enatos)

Tenth: δέκατος (dekatos)

These are used in everyday contexts, such as dates and rankings.
For instance, if you're talking about the first of May, you would say,
"η πρώτη Μαΐου" (i proti Maiou). Or if you're discussing the third
person in line, you would say, "ο τρίτος στη σειρά" (o tritos sti seira).

Understanding these ordinal numbers can help you navigate various scenarios, from scheduling appointments to discussing events.

Counting Exercises

To solidify your understanding, let's do some counting exercises. Fill in the blanks with the correct numbers:

1. _____ μήλα (five apples)

2. _____ σπίτια (three houses)

3. _____ βιβλία (seven books)

Matching numbers to words can also be helpful. Match the Greek number to its English equivalent:

1. Είκοσι πέντε   a. 25

2. τριάντα επτά   b. 37

3. εξήντα δύο   c. 62

Listening to audio exercises can further reinforce your learning. Practice by repeating numbers after hearing them. This will improve your pronunciation and help you remember the numbers more effectively.

Practical Applications

Numbers are helpful in many practical scenarios. When shopping, you'll frequently need to know prices and quantities. For example, if something costs 20 euros, you would say, "Κοστίζει είκοσι ευρώ" (Kostizei eikosi evro). When buying multiple items, like ten oranges, you might say, "Δέκα πορτοκάλια, παρακαλώ" (Deka portokalia, parakalo).

Telling time is another essential skill. If it's 3:30, you would say, "Είναι τρεις και μισή" (Einai treis kai misi). Knowing how to ask and give the time can be helpful in daily interactions.

Lastly, knowing how to give and ask for phone numbers is crucial. You might say, "Ποιο είναι το τηλέφωνό σας;" (Poio einai to tilefono sas?) when asking for someone's number. Giving your number might sound like, "Το τηλέφωνό μου είναι τρία, τέσσερα, πέντε, έξι, επτά, οκτώ" (To tilefono mou einai tria, tessera, pente, eksi, epta, okto).

Mastering numbers and basic counting in Greek will significantly enhance your ability to navigate everyday situations. Whether you're shopping, telling time, or giving your phone number, these skills are essential for effective communication. Practice regularly, and soon, you'll find these numbers rolling off your tongue with ease.

1.6 Days of the Week and Months of the Year

Learning the days of the week and months of the year in Greek is not just about memorizing words; it's about understanding how these terms fit into daily life. The days of the week are essential for planning activities, making appointments, and understanding schedules. Here are the days of the week in Greek, along with their phonetic transcriptions:

- Monday: Δευτέρα (Deftera)

- Tuesday: Τρίτη (Triti)

- Wednesday: Τετάρτη (Tetarti)

- Thursday: Πέμπτη (Pempti)

- Friday: Παρασκευή (Paraskevi)

- Saturday: Σάββατο (Savvato)

- Sunday: Κυριακή (Kyriaki)

Each day has its unique pronunciation. For example, Δευτέρα starts with a "th" sound, similar to the "th" in "this," while Κυριακή has a stress on the last syllable. To help with pronunciation, you can find audio clips online where native speakers pronounce each day. Listening and repeating these clips will help you get the correct intonation and stress.

Understanding days in context can make them easier to remember. For instance, you might say, "Τα λέμε τη Δευτέρα" (See you on Monday) when making plans. Or, if you're looking forward to the weekend, you might say, "Ανυπομονώ για το Σάββατο" (I can't wait for Saturday). Using these phrases in your daily conversations will help reinforce your learning.

Next, let's move on to the months of the year. Here are the months in Greek with their phonetic transcriptions:

- January: Ιανουάριος (Ianouarios)

- February: Φεβρουάριος (Fevrouarios)

- March: Μάρτιος (Martios)

- April: Απρίλιος (Aprilios)

- May: Μάιος (Maios)

- June: Ιούνιος (Iounios)

- July: Ιούλιος (Ioulios)

- August: Αύγουστος (Avgoustos)

- September: Σεπτέμβριος (Septemvrios)

- October: Οκτώβριος (Oktovrios)

- November: Νοέμβριος (Noemvrios)

- December: Δεκέμβριος (Dekemvrios)

Pronouncing these months can be tricky, especially with the unique Greek sounds. For instance, Ιανουάριος has a smooth flow, while Σεπτέμβριος has a stress on the second syllable. Again, audio resources can be beneficial. Listen to native speakers and practice saying the months out loud.

Greek holidays and seasons add another layer of understanding. For example, Easter, known as Πάσχα (Pascha), is one of the most significant holidays in Greece and usually falls in April. Knowing the months helps you understand and participate in these cultural events. Similarly, understanding the seasonal context, like "Άνοιξη" (Spring) or "Χειμώνας" (Winter), can enrich your conversations and experiences in Greece.

Writing and saying dates in Greek follows a specific format. Typically, the day comes first, followed by the month and year. For example, April 5th, 2023, would be written as "5 Απριλίου 2023." In spoken Greek, you might say, "Πέμπτη Απριλίου δύο χιλιάδες είκοσι τρία" (Pempti Aprilíou dýo chiliádes eíkosi tría). This format is consistent and straightforward once you get the hang of it.

To reinforce your learning, practice writing dates in different contexts. For birthdays, you might write, "Τα γενέθλιά μου είναι στις 15 Ιουλίου" (My birthday is on July 15th). For appointments, you could write, "Έχω ραντεβού στις 3 Μαρτίου" (I have an appointment on March 3rd). These exercises will help you become more comfortable with dates in Greek.

Practice Activities

Interactive activities can make learning more engaging. Try matching days and months to pictures that represent them. For instance, match a picture of a snowy landscape with "Δεκέμβριος" (December) or a beach scene with "Αύγουστος" (August). Fill-in-the-blank exercises can also be helpful. For example, "Το ραντεβού μου είναι στις _____" (My appointment is on ____), where you fill in the correct date. Audio exercises where you listen to dates and repeat them can further reinforce your skills.

By mastering the days of the week and months of the year, you'll find it easier to plan your activities, understand schedules, and participate in conversations. This foundational knowledge will serve you well as you continue to learn Greek. Consistent practice, listening to native speakers, and using these terms in real-life contexts will help solidify your understanding and improve your fluency.

Chapter 2: Essential Grammar Basics

When I began studying Greek, I was struck by how different the grammar was from English. This chapter aims to break down Greek grammar into manageable parts, starting with subject pronouns and basic sentence structure.

2.1 Subject Pronouns and Basic Sentence Structure

Greek subject pronouns are the building blocks of sentences, and mastering them is critical to constructing clear, meaningful sentences. Greek, like English, uses subject pronouns to indicate who is acting as the verb. The Greek subject pronouns are as follows:

- Εγώ (I)

- Εσύ (you, singular informal)

- Αυτός/αυτή/αυτό (he/she/it)

- Εμείς (we)

- Εσείς (you, plural or formal)

- Αυτοί/αυτές/αυτά (they)

Unlike English, which frequently uses subject pronouns, Greek often omits them because the verb conjugations already indicate the subject. However, pronouns are used to emphasize or avoid ambiguity. Let's look at each pronoun in detail. Εγώ means "I" and is used to emphasize the speaker, as in "Εγώ μαθαίνω Ελληνικά" (I am learning Greek). Εσύ is the informal singular "you," often used among friends and family, as in "Εσύ διαβάζεις" (You read). Αυτός, αυτή, and αυτό mean "he," "she," and "it," respectively. For example, "Αυτός είναι δάσκαλος" (He is a teacher), "Αυτή τρέχει" (She runs), and "Αυτό είναι βιβλίο" (It is a book). Εμείς translates to "we," used in sentences like "Εμείς πηγαίνουμε στο πάρκο" (We are going to the park). Εσείς can mean "you" in both plural and formal contexts, as in "Εσείς μιλάτε Ελληνικά" (You speak Greek). Lastly, αυτοί, αυτές, and αυτά mean "they," with αυτοί used for masculine or mixed groups, αυτές for feminine groups, and αυτά for neuter groups. For instance, "Αυτοί παίζουν" (They play - masculine or mixed group), "Αυτές μαγειρεύουν" (They cook - feminine group), and "Αυτά είναι παιχνίδια" (They are toys - neuter group).

Understanding basic sentence structure in Greek involves learning the Subject-Verb-Object (SVO) order, similar to English. This means the subject comes first, followed by the verb, and then the object. For example, "Εγώ διαβάζω βιβλίο" translates to "I read a book," where "εγώ" is the subject, "διαβάζω" is the verb, and "βιβλίο" is the object. This structure provides a clear and straightforward way to construct sentences. However, Greek is flexible with word order, especially for emphasis. For instance, "Βιβλίο διαβάζω εγώ" still means "I read a book," but emphasizes "βιβλίο" (book).

Verb agreement is essential for correct sentence formation. In Greek, verbs change form based on the subject pronoun. For example, the verb "to read" is "διαβάζω." Conjugated with different pronouns, it becomes "εγώ διαβάζω" (I read), "εσύ διαβάζεις" (you read), "αυτός/αυτή/αυτό διαβάζει" (he/she/it reads), "εμείς διαβάζουμε" (we read), "εσείς διαβάζετε" (you read), and "αυτοί/αυτές/αυτά διαβάζουν" (they read). Notice how the verb endings change to match the subject pronoun. This agreement between the subject and verb is crucial for clarity and correctness in Greek sentences.

To reinforce your understanding, let's practice with some exercises. Try filling in the blanks in the following sentences with the correct pronoun and verb form:

1. _____ (I) μαθαίνω Ελληνικά.

2. _____ (You, singular informal) τρέχεις στο πάρκο.

3. _____ (He) είναι δάσκαλος.

4. _____ (We) πηγαίνουμε στο σχολείο.

5. _____ (You, plural/formal) μιλάτε Ισπανικά.

6. _____ (They, masculine or mixed group) παίζουν ποδόσφαιρο.

Matching pronouns to verbs is another effective exercise. For instance, match the pronoun "εμείς" with the correct verb form "πηγαίνουμε" (we go). Finally, try constructing simple sentences using the SVO structure. For example, use "εγώ" and "μαγειρεύω" (to cook) to form "Εγώ μαγειρεύω φαγητό" (I cook food).

Mastering subject pronouns and basic sentence structure lays a solid foundation for further learning. These elements are the building blocks of communication, enabling you to express yourself clearly and accurately in Greek. Practice regularly, and soon, constructing sentences becomes second nature.

2.2 Present Tense Verb Conjugations

Understanding verb conjugations in the present tense is crucial for forming accurate sentences in Greek. Regular verbs follow predictable patterns, making them easier to learn. Let's start with the two main types of regular verbs: -ω and -ώ verbs. For -ω verbs, such as "αγαπώ" (to love), the conjugation pattern is consistent. Here's a conjugation table for "αγαπώ":

εγώ αγαπώ (I love)

εσύ αγαπάς (you love)

αυτός/αυτή/αυτό αγαπά (he/she/it loves)

εμείς αγαπάμε (we love)

εσείς αγαπάτε (you love)

αυτοί/αυτές/αυτά αγαπάνε (they love)

Similarly, -ώ verbs like "μπορώ" (to be able) follow a regular pattern. Here's how "μπορώ" conjugates:

εγώ μπορώ (I can)

εσύ μπορείς (you can)

αυτός/αυτή/αυτό μπορεί (he/she/it can)

εμείς μπορούμε (we can)

εσείς μπορείτε (you can)

αυτοί/αυτές/αυτά μπορούν (they can)

Notice the endings change based on the subject pronoun, which helps indicate who is acting. Regular verbs are your friends in Greek because once you learn the pattern, you can apply it to many other verbs.

Irregular verbs, on the other hand, don't follow these patterns and need to be memorized individually. Two of the most common irregular verbs are "είμαι" (to be) and "έχω" (to have). Here's how "είμαι" conjugates:

εγώ είμαι (I am)

εσύ είσαι (you are)

αυτός/αυτή/αυτό είναι (he/she/it is)

εμείς είμαστε (we are)

εσείς είστε (you are)

αυτοί/αυτές/αυτά είναι (they are)

For "έχω," the conjugation is as follows:

εγώ έχω (I have)

εσύ έχεις (you have)

αυτός/αυτή/αυτό έχει (he/she/it has)

εμείς έχουμε (we have)

εσείς έχετε (you have)

αυτοί/αυτές/αυτά έχουν (they have)

Using these irregular verbs in sentences can help solidify your understanding. For example, "Εγώ είμαι μαθητής" (I am a student) or "Αυτοί έχουν σπίτι" (They have a house). Practice sentences like these to become more comfortable with these irregular forms.

Forming negative sentences in Greek is straightforward. You place "δεν" before the verb. For instance, "Δεν διαβάζω" means "I do not read." This rule applies to both regular and irregular verbs. Here are more examples: "Δεν είμαι κουρασμένος" (I am not tired), "Δεν έχω αυτοκίνητο" (I do not have a car). This simple insertion of "δεν" changes the sentence's meaning to its negative form.

Let's engage in some practice activities to reinforce your understanding of present-tense conjugations. Start with conjugation drills for both regular and irregular verbs—for example, practice conjugating "αγαπώ" and "μπορώ" with different pronouns. Next, move on to sentence completion exercises. Fill in the blanks with the correct verb form: "Εγώ _____ (αγαπώ) τη μουσική." (I love music), "Εσύ _____ (μπορείς) να τρέξεις γρήγορα." (You can run fast).

Conjugation Practice Chart

Pronoun αγαπώ (to love)μπορώ (to be able)είμαι (to be)έχω (to have)

Εγώ αγαπώ μπορώ είμαι έχω

Εσύ αγαπάς μπορείς είσαι έχεις

Αυτός/αυτή/αυτό αγαπά μπορεί είναι έχει

Εμείς αγαπάμε μπορούμε είμαστε έχουμε

Εσείς αγαπάτεμπορείτε είστε έχετε

Αυτοί/αυτές/αυτά αγαπάνε μπορούν είναι έχουν

Listening and repeating exercises can also be very effective. Find audio recordings of native speakers and repeat them. This will help you get used to the rhythm and intonation of Greek verbs in the present tense. By practicing these exercises consistently, you'll find that conjugating verbs and forming sentences becomes second nature.

2.3 Definite and Indefinite Articles

Understanding definite and indefinite articles in Greek is fundamental to mastering the language. Greek articles, much like in English, help specify nouns. However, Greek articles are more complex because they must agree on gender, number, and case with the nouns they modify. Let's start with definite articles. The Greek definite articles are ο (masculine), η (feminine), and το (neuter).

For example, "ο άντρας" means "the man," "η γυναίκα" means "the woman," and "το παιδί" means "the child." These articles change when the nouns they accompany are plural. For instance, "ο άντρας" becomes "οι άντρες" (the men), "η γυναίκα" becomes "οι γυναίκες" (the women), and "το παιδί" becomes "τα παιδιά" (the children). Understanding this agreement is crucial for constructing grammatically correct sentences. Consider the sentence "Ο δάσκαλος διδάσκει" (The teacher teaches). Here, "ο" agrees with "δάσκαλος" in gender (masculine) and number (singular). Change the noun to plural, and the sentence becomes "Οι δάσκαλοι διδάσκουν" (The teachers teach), with "οι" now agreeing with the plural noun "δάσκαλοι."

Indefinite articles in Greek function similarly to the English "a" or "an," but they also must agree in gender. The Greek indefinite articles are ένας (masculine), μία (feminine), and ένα (neuter). For example, "ένας άντρας" means "a man," "μία γυναίκα" means "a woman," and "ένα παιδί" means "a child." These articles are used when referring to non-specific items or people. For instance, "Βλέπω έναν άνθρωπο" (I see a man) uses "έναν" (the accusative form of "ένας") to indicate that the man is not a specific individual known to the speaker. However, when specificity is apparent, the definite article is used: "Βλέπω τον άνθρωπο" (I see the man).

One interesting aspect of Greek is when articles are omitted. Unlike English, Greek sometimes drops the article in specific contexts, especially everyday speech. For example, in a sentence like "Πίνω καφέ" (I drink coffee), the article "ένα" (a) is omitted even though it is understood that the speaker is referring to a single, non-specific coffee. This omission is more familiar with indefinite articles and in informal settings.

To understand how articles agree with the gender and number of nouns, let's look at some examples. Gender-specific examples include "ο άντρας" (the man) for masculine, "η γυναίκα" (the woman) for feminine, and "το παιδί" (the child) for neuter. When these nouns become plural, they change to "οι άντρες" (the men), "οι γυναίκες" (the women), and "τα παιδιά" (the children), respectively. The articles change to match the gender and number of the nouns they modify. This agreement is consistent across different cases, such as nominative, accusative, and genitive.

Let's practice with some exercises to reinforce your understanding. Try filling in the blanks with the correct article:

1. _____ (the) βιβλίο (book) είναι ενδιαφέρον.

2. _____ (a) γάτα (cat) κοιμάται.

3. _____ (the) παιδιά (children) παίζουν.

Matching articles to nouns can also be helpful. For example, match "ο" with "άντρας," "η" with "γυναίκα," and "το" with "παιδί." Constructing sentences with both definite and indefinite articles will further solidify your understanding. Try making sentences like "Ο δάσκαλος διαβάζει ένα βιβλίο" (The teacher reads a book) or "Η γυναίκα βλέπει τον σκύλο" (The woman sees the dog).

You'll find your Greek sentences becoming more precise and accurate by mastering definite and indefinite articles. These small words might seem insignificant, but they are crucial in conveying the proper meaning and context. Practice regularly, and soon, using the correct articles will become second nature.

2.4 Basic Noun Cases and Their Uses

When I first encountered Greek noun cases, I felt like stepping into a new world of grammar rules. These noun cases determine the role of a noun in a sentence, and understanding them is crucial for clear communication. Let's start with the nominative case used for the sentence's subject. For example, in the sentence "Ο μαθητής διαβάζει" (The student reads), "Ο μαθητής" (the student) is in the nominative case. This case identifies who or what is acting. More examples include "Η γυναίκα μαγειρεύει" (The woman cooks) and "Το παιδί παίζει" (The child plays). The nominative case is straightforward and forms the basis for understanding other cases.

Next, the accusative case is used for the sentence's direct object. This case answers the question "whom" or "what" after the verb. For instance, in "Βλέπω τον άντρα" (I see the man), "τον άντρα" (the man) is in the accusative case, indicating that the man is the direct object of the verb "βλέπω" (see). Other examples include "Διαβάζω το βιβλίο" (I read the book) and "Ακούω τη μουσική" (I listen to the music). The accusative case is essential for specifying the receiver of the action, making your sentences clear and precise.

The genitive case, on the other hand, indicates possession and relationships. It answers the question "whose" or "of what." For example, in "το βιβλίο του παιδιού" (the child's book), "του παιδιού" (the child's) is in the genitive case, showing that the book belongs to the child. This case is also used for relationships, such as "η μητέρα του φίλου μου" (my friend's mother). Other examples include "το σπίτι της Μαρίας" (Maria's house) and "η πόρτα του αυτοκινήτου" (the car's door). Understanding the genitive case helps you express ownership and relationships clearly and effectively.

To practice these noun cases, let's start with some identification exercises. Look at the following sentences and identify the case of the underlined nouns:

1. Ο δάσκαλος διδάσκει τους μαθητές. (The teacher teaches the students.)

2. Το ποδήλατο της Μαρίας είναι κόκκινο. (Maria's bicycle is red.)

3. Βλέπω μια ταινία στον κινηματογράφο. (I watch a movie at the cinema.)

Next, try transforming sentences from one case to another. For example, convert the nominative "Ο δάσκαλος" (The teacher) to the accusative "Τον δάσκαλο" (The teacher as the direct object). Here are some sentences to practice:

1. Η γυναίκα αγοράζει το ψωμί. (The woman buys the bread.)

2. Το παιδί παίζει με το σκύλο. (The child plays with the dog.)

3. Ο άντρας διαβάζει την εφημερίδα. (The man reads the newspaper.)

Finally, let's do some fill-in-the-blank exercises to reinforce your understanding. Fill in the blanks with the correct noun case:

1. _____ (The teacher) διδάσκει _____ (the students).

2. _____ (Maria's) ποδήλατο είναι κόκκινο.

3. Βλέπω _____ (a movie) στον κινηματογράφο.

Mastering these primary noun cases will significantly enhance your ability to form accurate and meaningful sentences in Greek. Whether talking about your friend's new car or describing who is reading a book, understanding these cases will make your Greek more precise and expressive.

2.5 Adjectives and Agreement

When I first encountered Greek adjectives, I was struck by how they added color and detail to sentences. Adjectives in Greek must agree with the nouns they describe in gender, number, and case. This agreement makes sentences more precise and expressive. Let's start with the basics. Greek adjectives change their endings to match the gender of the noun. For example, the adjective "καλός" (good) has different forms: "καλός" (masculine), "καλή" (feminine), and "καλό" (neuter). You must be mindful of the noun's gender when choosing the appropriate adjective form.

Common adjectives and their forms include "μικρός" (small), "μεγάλος" (big), and "όμορφος" (beautiful). For example, "μικρός" becomes "μικρή" for feminine and "μικρό" for neuter. In a sentence, you might say "ο μικρός σκύλος" (the small dog) for a masculine noun, "η μικρή γάτα" (the small cat) for a feminine noun, and "το μικρό σπίτι" (the small house) for a neuter noun. These examples show how the adjective changes to match the noun it describes, creating a cohesive and understandable sentence.

Forming comparative and superlative adjectives in Greek is straightforward once you know the rules. To form comparatives, you generally add the suffix "-τερος" to the adjective. For example, "μεγάλος" (big) becomes "μεγαλύτερος" (bigger). To make it superlative, you use the definite article

skylos

"o" before the adjective and the suffix "-τατος." So, "μεγαλύτερος" (bigger) becomes "ο μεγαλύτερος" (the biggest). In sentences, you might say, "Αυτό το σπίτι είναι μεγαλύτερο" (This house is bigger) for the comparative form or "Αυτό είναι το μεγαλύτερο σπίτι" (This is the biggest house) for the superlative form. These forms help you compare and emphasize qualities, making your descriptions more vivid.

gata

The position of adjectives in Greek sentences can change their meaning slightly. In an attributive position, the adjective comes before the noun, as in "ο καλός άνθρωπος" (the good man). In the predicative position, the adjective comes after the verb "to be," as in "ο άνθρωπος είναι καλός" (the man is good). Understanding these positions helps you structure your sentences correctly and convey your intended meaning. For example, "η όμορφη γυναίκα" (the beautiful woman) vs. "η γυναίκα είναι όμορφη" (the woman is beautiful). Both sentences describe a beautiful woman, but the placement of the adjective changes the sentence structure.

Let's practice with some exercises to reinforce your understanding of adjectives and their agreement. Start by matching adjectives to nouns. For example, pair "μικρός" with "σκύλος" (dog), "μικρή" with "γάτα" (cat), and "μικρό" with "σπίτι" (house). Next, try completing sentences with the correct adjective form: "Ο _____ (small) σκύλος κοιμάται" (The small dog is sleeping). Fill in the blank with "μικρός."

Adjective Agreement Practice

Noun Adjective (small)Adjective (big)Adjective (beautiful)

Σκύλος μικρός μεγάλος όμορφος

Γάτα μικρή μεγάλη όμορφη

Σπίτι μικρό μεγάλο όμορφο

For comparative and superlative practice, try forming sentences using both forms. For example, "Αυτό το βιβλίο είναι _____ (more

interesting)" (This book is more interesting). Fill in the blank with
"πιο ενδιαφέρον." For the superlative, you might say, "Αυτό είναι το πιο
ενδιαφέρον βιβλίο" (This is the most interesting book). These exercises
will help you become comfortable using adjectives in various contexts,
making your Greek more expressive and accurate.

2.6 Questions and Negations

Forming questions in Greek can initially seem challenging, but with
some practice, it becomes intuitive. Starting with yes/no questions
these are formed by simply raising the intonation at the end of the
sentence, much like in English. For instance, to ask, "Do you read the
book?" in Greek, you would say, "Διαβάζεις το βιβλίο;" Notice how the
structure remains the same as a statement, but the intonation changes.
This simple method applies to many yes/no questions, making it easy
to ask basic inquiries.

Wh- questions, on the other hand, require specific question words.
These include "Ποιος" (Who), "Τι" (What), "Πότε" (When), "Πού"
(Where), and "Γιατί" (Why). To form these questions, you place the
question word at the beginning of the sentence. For example, "Ποιος
διαβάζει το βιβλίο;" means "Who reads the book?" Similarly, "Τι κάνεις;"
translates to "What are you doing?" These question words are essential
for gathering detailed information. Using them frequently will help
you become more comfortable with their structure and usage.

In Greek, forming negative sentences is relatively straightforward.
The word "δεν" is placed before the verb to negate the action. For
example, "I do not see" translates to "Δεν βλέπω." This rule is consistent
across different verbs and tenses, making it easy to remember. Consider the sentence "Δεν πηγαίνω στο σχολείο" (I do not go to school).
Here, "δεν" negates the verb "πηγαίνω" (to go). This simple addition

changes the entire meaning of the sentence, allowing you to express negation clearly and effectively.

Let's delve deeper into crucial question words and their uses. "Ποιος" (Who) is used to inquire about a person. For instance, "Ποιος είναι αυτός;" means "Who is he?" The word "Τι" (What) is used for objects or actions, as in "Τι θέλεις;" (What do you want?). "Πότε" (When) is used to ask about time, such as "Πότε φεύγεις;" (When are you leaving?). "Πού" (Where) inquires about location, for example, "Πού μένεις;" (Where do you live?). Lastly, "Γιατί" (Why) is used to ask for reasons, like "Γιατί είσαι εδώ;" (Why are you here?). These words are fundamental for constructing a wide range of questions, enabling you to gather more detailed information in conversations.

To reinforce your understanding, let's practice forming questions and negations. Start by creating questions from statements. For example, turn the statement "Διαβάζεις το βιβλίο" (You read the book) into the question "Διαβάζεις το βιβλίο;" (Do you read the book?). Next, try transforming positive sentences into negative ones. Take "Βλέπω τη γάτα" (I see the cat) and change it to "Δεν βλέπω τη γάτα" (I do not see the cat).

Practice Exercise: Fill in the Blanks

1. _____ (Why) είσαι εδώ; (Why are you here?)

2. _____ (Where) πηγαίνεις; (Where are you going?)

3. Δεν _____ (read) το βιβλίο. (I do not read the book.)

These exercises will help you become proficient in forming questions and negations. Practicing regularly will reinforce these concepts, making it easier to use them in everyday conversations. By mastering these basic structures, you'll be well-equipped to ask questions and express negation in Greek confidently.

Understanding how to form questions and negations is a crucial skill in any language. It allows you to gather information, clarify misunderstandings, and express yourself more accurately. As you continue to practice, these structures will become second nature, greatly enhancing your ability to communicate in Greek. These tools allow you to easily navigate conversational scenarios, asking questions and negating statements as needed. Keep practicing, and soon, you'll find yourself using these structures effortlessly.

Chapter 3: Daily Life Vocabulary

This chapter aims to equip you with the vocabulary to navigate these everyday situations confidently, starting with food and dining.

3.1 Food and Dining Vocabulary

portokali

Understanding basic food vocabulary can make your dining experiences in Greece enjoyable and stress-free. Let's start with some everyday food items. Fruits like "μήλο" (apple) and "πορτοκάλι" (orange) are staples you'll find in markets and on menus. Vegetables are just as important, with "ντομάτα" (tomato) and "κρεμμύδι" (onion) frequently appearing in salads and cooked dishes. Knowing these basic terms can help you identify ingredients and make informed choices about what to eat.

Protein sources are another crucial part of the Greek diet. "Κοτόπουλο" (chicken) and "ψάρι" (fish) are standard options you'll encounter. Whether you're ordering a "σουβλάκι" (skewer) with chicken or a grilled fish, these words will be helpful. Additionally, dishes like "αρνί" (lamb) and

domata

"μοσχάρι" (veal) are popular, especially during festive occasions. Understanding these terms will help you navigate menus and make choices that suit your taste and dietary preferences.

Dining out in Greece is a social affair; knowing some key phrases can enhance your experience. When you're ready to order, you might say, "Θα ήθελα..." (I would like...), followed by your chosen dish. For instance, "Θα ήθελα μια σαλάτα" (I would like a salad). This phrase is versatile and can be

kremmydi

used for anything on the menu. Once you've enjoyed your meal and are ready to pay, asking for the bill is simple with "Τον λογαριασμό, παρακαλώ" (The bill, please). These phrases are essential for a smooth dining experience and show a level of respect and effort that locals appreciate.

Menus in Greece often feature various items, from appetizers to main courses. Everyday menu items include "σαλάτα" (salad) and "κυρίως πιάτο" (main course). For example, you might see "Χωριάτικη σαλάτα" (Greek salad) or "Μουσακάς" (moussaka) listed. Familiarizing yourself with these terms

kotopoylo

can help you understand what you're ordering and ensure you enjoy your meal. Additionally, knowing how to ask questions about the menu, such as "Τι είναι αυτό;" (What is this?), can help you navigate unfamiliar dishes.

Communicating dietary preferences and restrictions is crucial, especially if you have specific needs. If you're vegetarian, you can say, "Είμαι χορτοφάγος" (I am vegetarian). This phrase can help you find suitable options on the menu. For those with allergies, "Έχω αλλεργία στα καρύδια" (I

moussaka

am allergic to nuts) is an important phrase to remember. Knowing how to express these needs clearly can ensure you enjoy your meal without issues.

Dining etiquette in Greece involves more than just knowing what to say. Sharing dishes, known as "μεζέδες" (small dishes for sharing), is a common practice. It's an opportunity to try various foods and engage in a communal dining experience. Tipping is another essential aspect. While not obligatory, leaving a small tip is customary if you've enjoyed your meal and service. Finally, table manners like waiting for everyone to be served before starting to eat and using utensils properly are appreciated and show respect for local customs.

Understanding these aspects of food and dining vocabulary will make your meals in Greece more enjoyable and less stressful. Whether you're ordering a simple "σουβλάκι" or navigating a multi-course meal, these words and phrases will help you communicate effectively and appreciate Greece's rich culinary traditions. Learning and using this vocabulary will enhance your dining experiences and show your respect for Greek culture and hospitality.

3.2 Shopping and Market Vocabulary

Shopping in Greece presents a unique opportunity to immerse yourself in daily life, engage with locals, and practice your Greek. Knowing some key phrases can make the experience smoother and more enjoyable. When you enter a shop and find something you like, you might ask, "Πόσο κοστίζει;" (How much does it cost?). This simple question can help you quickly determine if an item fits your budget. If you're shopping for clothes or shoes, it's helpful to know how to ask, "Μπορώ να το δοκιμάσω;" (Can I try it on?). This phrase is essential for ensuring that what you buy fits well. Another handy phrase is "'Έχετε..." (Do you have...), which you can use to inquire about specific items. For instance, "'Έχετε αυτό σε άλλο χρώμα;" (Do you have this in another color?).

Understanding the different types of markets in Greece can enhance your shopping experience. Supermarkets, or "σούπερ μάρκετ," are where you'll find a wide range of groceries and household items. These are similar to supermarkets you might be used to, offering everything from fresh produce to cleaning supplies. On the other hand, farmer's markets, known as "λαϊκή αγορά," offer a more traditional shopping experience. Here, you can find fresh fruits, vegetables, and local delicacies directly from the producers. Specialty stores like "αρτοποιείο" (bakery) and "κρεοπωλείο" (butcher shop) provide specific items and often feature high-quality, fresh products. These shops are great places to find freshly baked bread, pastries, and various cuts of meat.

Describing products accurately can help you get precisely what you want when shopping. Knowing how to discuss sizes and quantities is crucial. For example, if you need something small, you can say "μικρό," while "μεγάλο" means large. If you're looking for fresh produce, "φρέσκο" (fresh) is the word to use, and "καινούργιο" (new) is useful when asking about new arrivals or recent stock. Additionally, asking for recommendations can lead you to discover new products. Phrases like "Τι προτείνετε;" (What do you recommend?) can open up conversations with shopkeepers who are often eager to share their knowledge and favorite items.

Understanding payment and transactions is essential. In Greece, you'll often be asked if you're paying "μετρητά ή κάρτα;" (cash or card?). This phrase is vital for completing your purchase. If you need a receipt, ask, "Μπορώ να έχω μια απόδειξη;" (Can I have a receipt?). This is especially useful for keeping track of your spending or needing proof of purchase. Sometimes, you might need to return or exchange an item. Knowing how to explain this can save you a lot of trouble. Say, "Θα ήθελα να το επιστρέψω" (I would like to return this) or "Μπορώ να το αλλάξω;" (Can I exchange this?). These phrases ensure clear communication with the shop staff, smoothing the process.

Shopping in Greece is not just about buying things; it's about engaging with the culture and people. Greeting shopkeepers with a friendly "Καλημέρα" (Good morning) or "Καλησπέρα" (Good evening) can make a big difference. Establishing rapport with store employees often leads to valuable local recommendations and a more enjoyable shopping experience. Whether you're at a bustling "λαϊκή αγορά" or a quiet "αρτοποιείο," these interactions make your shopping experience richer and more meaningful. Understanding these shopping phrases and vocabulary will help you confidently navigate different markets and stores, making your time in Greece more enjoyable and productive.

3.3 Directions and Transportation

Navigating a new place can be daunting, especially when unfamiliar with the language. Knowing how to ask for and give directions can make a huge difference. When you need to find your way, ask "Πώς πάω στο..." (How do I get to...) is a great start-

leophorio

ing point. For example, "Πώς πάω στο μουσείο;" (How do I get to the museum?). If you need to know the location of something, "Πού είναι το..." (Where is the...) is essential. For instance, "Πού είναι το φαρμακείο;" (Where is the pharmacy?). These phrases are your gateway to exploring new areas with confidence.

Understanding key directional words is crucial for following and giving directions. Knowing terms like "αριστερά" (left) and "δεξιά" (right) helps you navigate more easily. For example, someone might tell you, "Στρίψε αριστερά μετά τη γωνία" (Turn left after the corner) or "Πήγαινε δεξιά

treno

στο φανάρι" (Go right at the traffic light). Other useful words include "ευθεία" (straight) and "πίσω" (back), making it easier to follow complex directions. With these words in your vocabulary, you'll be more confident asking for and understanding directions.

Transportation vocabulary is another critical area. Knowing the words for different modes of transportation will make getting around much more straightforward. For instance, "λεωφορείο" (bus), "τρένο" (train), and "ταξί" (taxi) are fundamental. If you need to take the bus, you might ask,

taxi

"Πού είναι η στάση του λεωφορείου;" (Where is the bus stop?). Similarly, if you're looking to catch a train, "Πού είναι ο σταθμός του τρένου;" (Where is the train station?) will be helpful. These words and phrases are essential for navigating public transport and will serve you well in various situations.

Buying tickets and understanding how to navigate transportation systems can initially seem overwhelming, but it becomes manageable with a few key phrases. When purchasing a ticket, you can say, "'Ένα εισιτήριο για..." (A ticket to...), followed by your destination. For example, "'Ένα εισιτήριο για την Αθήνα, παρακαλώ" (A ticket to Athens, please). Understanding schedules and timetables is also crucial. Look for signs that say "Πρόγραμμα" (Schedule) and "Ωράριο" (Timetable) to find departure times. Common phrases for use in stations and stops include "Πότε φεύγει το επόμενο τρένο;" (When does the next train leave?) and "Ποια είναι η επόμενη στάση;" (What is the next stop?). These phrases will help you navigate transportation systems more effectively.

In case of emergencies, knowing how to communicate your needs is vital. If you miss your bus, you might say, "'Έχασα το λεωφορείο" (I missed the bus). If you find yourself in a difficult situation, "Χρειάζομαι βοήθεια" (I need help) is a crucial phrase. Contacting transportation authorities can also be necessary. For instance, "Πώς μπορώ να επικοινωνήσω με τις αρχές μεταφοράς;" (How can I contact the transportation authorities?) can be extremely useful. Being prepared with these phrases ensures you can handle unexpected public transport situations.

Navigating Greece becomes much simpler when you can ask for and understand directions, use transportation vocabulary effectively, buy tickets, and handle emergencies. These skills will make your travels smoother and more enjoyable, allowing you to focus on the experience rather than the logistics. With consistent practice and using these phrases, you'll move around quickly and confidently.

3.4 Travel and Accommodation Phrases

Booking a place to stay in Greece can be straightforward once you know the correct vocabulary and phrases. Understanding different types of accommodation is a good starting point. If you're looking for a hotel, you'll want to use the word "ξενοδοχείο." For a more intimate setting, perhaps a guesthouse, the word "ξενώνας" will be helpful. When making a reservation, you can say, "Θα ήθελα να κάνω μια κράτηση" (I would like to make a reservation). This phrase is versatile and can be used for any accommodation. Additionally, asking about amenities is essential to ensure your stay is comfortable. Phrases like "Υπάρχει Wi-Fi;" (Is there Wi-Fi?) or "Έχετε πρωινό;" (Do you have breakfast?) can help you gather the information you need.

Checking in and out of your accommodation involves critical phrases that can smooth the process. Upon arrival, you might approach the front desk and say, "Έχω μια κράτηση" (I have a reservation), followed by your name or reservation details. Don't hesitate to ask if you need assistance with your luggage or directions to your room. When it's time to leave, you'll want to use the phrase, "Θα ήθελα να κάνω check-out" (I would like to check out). If you need a bit more time, asking for a late check-out can be done by saying, "Μπορώ να κάνω αργοπορημένο check-out;" (Can I have a late check-out?). These phrases ensure that your check-in and check-out experiences are hassle-free.

When traveling, having a few essential phrases in your repertoire can make navigating new places much more accessible. Asking for recommendations is a great way to discover local gems. You can say, "Τι μου προτείνετε να δω;" (What do you recommend I see?). This helps you find interesting places and opens up a conversation with locals, who are often eager to share their favorite spots. Inquiring about tours can also enhance your travel experience. Phrases like "Υπάρχουν ξεναγήσεις;" (Are there tours?) can provide you with information about guided tours that offer more profound insights into the area's history and culture.

Dealing with travel issues is an inevitable part of any trip, and knowing how to address them in Greek can make a big difference. If you find yourself in the unfortunate situation of losing your luggage, you can say, "Έχασα τις αποσκευές μου" (I lost my luggage). This phrase can help you communicate your problem to airline staff or hotel personnel. Room problems can also arise, and expressing your concerns politely is crucial. If your room is too noisy, you might say, "Το δωμάτιο μου είναι πολύ θορυβώδες" (My room is very noisy). If the issue persists, asking for a change of room can be done by saying, "Μπορώ να αλλάξω δωμάτιο;" (Can I change rooms?). These phrases ensure that your concerns are addressed promptly, allowing you to enjoy your stay.

Having these travel and accommodation phrases at your disposal can significantly enhance your experience in Greece. They make practical tasks more manageable and enable you to engage with the local culture deeply. Whether you're booking a cozy "ξενώνας" or dealing with a noisy room, these phrases provide you with the tools to handle various situations confidently. Practice them regularly, and soon, you'll find yourself quickly navigating accommodation and travel-related scenarios, making your trip to Greece more enjoyable and stress-free.

3.5 Health and Emergency Vocabulary

Understanding words for body parts can be incredibly useful during a medical visit. For example, "κεφάλι" means head, and "χέρι" means hand. Knowing these terms can help you describe symptoms accurately. Common symptoms you might need to express include "πονοκέφαλος" (headache) and "πυρετός" (fever). These words are essential for communicating your condition to healthcare professionals.

Health professionals you may encounter include a "γιατρός" (doctor) and a "νοσοκόμα" (nurse). Familiarizing yourself with these terms can make a medical visit less intimidating.

In medical emergencies, knowing how to ask for help can be life-saving. If you urgently need medical assistance, you can say, "Χρειάζομαι γιατρό" (I need a doctor). Describing your symptoms clearly is crucial. For example, "Έχω πόνο στο στομάχι" means "I have a stomach ache." These phrases can help healthcare providers understand your condition quickly. It's also wise to have emergency contact numbers saved in your phone. Knowing whom to call in an emergency can provide peace of mind and ensure you get help swiftly. Always list emergency numbers, including local healthcare facilities and emergency services.

Visiting a pharmacy in Greece is another situation where specific vocabulary can be beneficial. When you need medication, you might ask, "Μπορώ να έχω ασπιρίνη;" (Can I have aspirin?). If you require something over-the-counter, such as cough medicine, you can say, "Χρειάζομαι κάτι για τον βήχα" (I need something for a cough). Understanding prescription requirements is also essential. In Greece, some medications require a prescription, which is known as "συνταγή" in Greek. Knowing how to explain your needs clearly can make your pharmacy visit more efficient and effective.

Health insurance vocabulary is crucial if you need medical care while in Greece. Asking about insurance coverage can be done by saying, "Καλύπτεται από την ασφάλεια μου;" (Is it covered by my insurance?). This question is essential for understanding what costs you might incur. Providing your insurance information clearly is also crucial. Phrases like "Η ασφάλεια μου είναι με την εταιρεία..." (My insurance is with the company...) can help you communicate effectively with healthcare providers. Understanding co-pays and deductibles is equally essential. Knowing these terms can help you navigate the financial aspects of healthcare more smoothly.

Understanding these health and emergency phrases can help you handle medical situations more confidently. Whether you're describing a symptom, asking for medication, or dealing with health insurance, these phrases are indispensable. Practice them regularly to ensure you're prepared for any health-related issues that may arise during your time in Greece.

3.6 Weather and Seasons

afixi

Understanding the weather is crucial, especially when exploring new places or planning activities. Greek weather vocabulary helps you navigate conversations and make plans efficiently. Standard weather terms like "ηλιόλουστος" (sunny) and "βροχερός" (rainy) are essential. Imagine you're planning a day out, and someone says, "Σήμερα είναι ηλιόλουστος" (Today is sunny). You know it's a perfect day for the beach. Conversely, "Αύριο θα είναι βροχερός" (Tomorrow will be rainy) might prompt you to consider indoor activities. Temperature descriptions are also vital. Words like "ζεστός" (hot) and "κρύος" (cold) help you describe how it feels outside. For example, "Σήμερα κάνει ζέστη" (Today it is hot) or "Αύριο θα είναι κρύο" (Tomorrow will be cold). These terms are straightforward but immensely useful.

Seasonal changes are another aspect of weather to consider. Knowing the words for different seasons can help you discuss long-term plans or chat about the time of year. "Άνοιξη" means spring, "καλοκαίρι" is summer, "φθινόπωρο" is autumn, and "χειμώνας" is winter. For instance, if

kalokairi

someone asks, "Πότε είναι η άνοιξη στην Ελλάδα;" (When is spring in Greece?), you can respond, "Η άνοιξη ξεκινάει τον Μάρτιο" (Spring starts in March). These terms help you understand and participate in conversations about seasonal activities, like festivals or holidays, making your experience richer.

Discussing the weather is an everyday conversation starter, and knowing how to ask about it is useful. You might ask, "Τι καιρό κάνει;" (What is the weather like?). This question is perfect for initiating small talk. Describing the current weather can also be helpful. If it's a hot day, you might

fthinoporo

say, "Σήμερα κάνει ζέστη" (Today it is hot), or if it's raining, you might mention, "Σήμερα βρέχει" (Today it is raining). Discussing weather preferences can lead to engaging conversations. You could say, "Μου αρέσει ο ηλιόλουστος καιρός" (I like sunny weather) or "Προτιμώ τον κρύο χειμώνα" (I prefer the cold winter). These phrases make your conversations more dynamic and relatable.

Understanding and discussing weather forecasts can help you plan your activities better. Critical phrases like "πρόγνωση καιρού" (weather forecast) are essential. When you hear, "Η πρόγνωση καιρού για αύριο είναι βροχερός" (The weather forecast for tomorrow is rainy), you know to plan

chimonas

accordingly. Common weather symbols, like a sun for sunny or a cloud with rain for rainy, are also helpful. These symbols make it easier to understand forecasts, even if your Greek isn't perfect yet. Planning activities based on the weather is crucial. For example, if the forecast says, "Αύριο θα κάνει ζέστη" (Tomorrow will be hot), you might plan a beach day. Conversely, if it says, "Θα έχει καταιγίδα" (There will be a storm), you might opt for indoor activities.

Weather-related emergencies are situations where knowing the correct vocabulary can be life-saving. If you need to seek shelter, you can say, "Χρειάζομαι καταφύγιο" (I need shelter). This phrase is crucial during severe weather conditions. Reporting severe weather is also essential. If you need to inform someone about a storm, you might say, "Υπάρχει καταιγίδα" (There is a storm). Contacting emergency services is another critical aspect. Knowing how to ask for help, like saying, "Χρειάζομαι βοήθεια" (I need help), can make a significant difference in emergencies.

Understanding these weather and season-related phrases will make your stay in Greece more comfortable and engaging. Whether planning a day out, discussing the weather with locals, or handling weather emergencies, these terms equip you for various situations. Being prepared with this vocabulary ensures you can enjoy your time in Greece to the fullest, regardless of the weather.

In the next chapter, we'll explore practical exercises to reinforce your learning and help you apply these phrases in real-life situations.

Chapter 4:
Conversational
Phrases

This chapter will equip you with essential phrases for introducing yourself, asking someone's name, and discussing occupations. These are critical for everyday interactions and forming new relationships.

4.1 Introducing Yourself and Others

Introducing yourself is often the first step in any conversation. It sets the tone and helps you connect with the person you speak to. In Greek, a simple way to introduce yourself is by saying, "Με λένε..." (My name is...), followed by your name. For example, "Με λένε Γιώργο" (My name is George). This phrase is straightforward to remember. Another helpful phrase is "Είμαι από..." (I am from...), which helps you share your background. For example, "Είμαι από την Αμερική" (I am from America). This provides context and can be a great conversation starter. If you're a student, you might say, "Είμαι μαθητής" for males or "Είμαι μαθήτρια" for females, which means "I am a student." These phrases are foundational and will help you introduce yourself in various settings.

When it comes to introducing others, the phrases are just as important. If you're with a friend, you can say, "Αυτός είναι ο φίλος μου, Γιάννης" (This is my friend, Yannis). For introducing a female friend or relative, you would say, "Αυτή είναι η αδερφή μου, Μαρία" (This is my sister, Maria). These introductions help provide clarity and context in a conversation. They also show respect and consideration for the people you're with. Knowing how to introduce others can make social interactions smoother and more enjoyable.

Asking someone's name is a natural part of getting to know someone. In Greek, you can ask, "Πώς σε λένε;" (What is your name?). This phrase is informal and perfect for casual settings. In more formal situations, you might use "Ποιο είναι το όνομά σας;" (What is your name? Formal). These questions show interest and help you engage more deeply with the person you're speaking to. When someone asks for your name, you can respond with "Με λένε..." followed by your name. Knowing these phrases ensures you can navigate introductions smoothly, whether in a casual or formal setting.

Discussing occupations is another common topic of conversation. Asking someone about their job can provide insight into their daily life and interests. You might ask, "Τι δουλειά κάνεις;" (What do you do for a living?). This question is a great way to learn more about someone. If someone asks you this question, you can respond with your occupation. For example, "Είμαι δάσκαλος" (I am a teacher) for males or "Είμαι δασκάλα" for females. If you work in an office, you might say, "Δουλεύω σε γραφείο" (I work in an office). These phrases help build rapport and understand the people you meet.

Interactive Exercise: Introduce Yourself

Take a moment to practice introducing yourself. Write down your responses to the following prompts in Greek:

1. My name is...

2. I am from...

3. I am a student.

For example:

1. Με λένε Άννα. (My name is Anna.)

2. Είμαι από την Αγγλία. (I am from England.)

3. Είμαι μαθήτρια. (I am a student.)

Practicing these phrases will help you feel more confident when introducing yourself in Greek.

Knowing these basic conversational phrases will significantly enhance your ability to communicate and connect with others. They provide a solid foundation for meaningful interactions, whether introducing yourself, asking someone's name, or discussing occupations. Practice them regularly, and soon, they will become second nature, making your conversations in Greek more fluent and enjoyable.

4.2 Asking for Help and Information

Navigating a new environment can be overwhelming, especially if you don't speak the language fluently. Knowing how to ask for help can make your experience much smoother. Imagine you're in a busy street in Athens, feeling lost. You can approach someone and ask, "Μπορείτε να με βοηθήσετε;" (Can you help me?). This phrase is polite and straightforward, clarifying that you need assistance. If you find your-self in a more urgent situation, perhaps feeling unwell or distressed, "Χρειάζομαι βοήθεια" (I need help) is direct and conveys the urgency of your need. These phrases are invaluable for any situation where you need assistance, whether asking for directions or finding a specific location. For instance, if you need to locate a pharmacy quickly, you might say, "Πού είναι το πλησιέστερο φαρμακείο;" (Where is the nearest pharmacy?). This phrase can guide you to essential services when you need them most.

Having the correct phrases at your disposal can save you time and stress when inquiring about locations. If you're trying to navigate public transportation, you might ask, "Πού είναι η στάση λεωφορείου;" (Where is the bus stop?). This simple question can help you find your way around the city. If you're exploring a new town and want to visit the main attractions, "Πώς πάω στο κέντρο της πόλης;" (How do I get to the city center?) is a helpful phrase. These questions are practical and demonstrate your willingness to engage with the local culture.

Seeking specific information can enhance your overall experience by making interactions more meaningful. For example, if you're plan-ning a visit to a museum, you should know its operating hours. You can ask, "Τι ώρα ανοίγει το μουσείο;" (What time does the museum open?). This phrase helps you plan your activities more effectively. Knowing how to ask for a phone number is crucial if you're trying to stay connected or need to contact someone. "Ποιο είναι το τηλέφωνο σας;" (What is your phone number?) is a straightforward way to get the information you need. Additionally, if you're exploring a new area and want to get a better sense of your surroundings, you might ask, "'Εχετε χάρτη της περιοχής;" (Do you have a map of the area?). These questions show you're proactive and interested in maximizing your time.

Clarifying information is essential when you're trying to understand instructions or directions. It's natural to miss details or need something repeated, especially in a new language. If someone gives you directions, and you need to hear them again, you can politely ask, "Μπορείτε να το επαναλάβετε παρακαλώ;" (Can you repeat that, please?). This phrase shows respect and ensures you get the information you need. Sometimes, you might still need further clarification even after something is repeated. In such cases, saying, "Δεν κατάλαβα, μπορείτε να το εξηγήσετε;" (I didn't understand, can you explain?) can help you get a clearer understanding. This phrase is handy in more complex situations where you need detailed information.

Interactive Exercise: Asking for Directions

Practice asking for directions with this exercise. Imagine you need to find the following places. Write down how you would ask for directions in Greek:

1. The nearest bus stop.

2. The city center.

3. A nearby pharmacy.

For example:

1. Πού είναι η στάση λεωφορείου; (Where is the bus stop?)

2. Πώς πάω στο κέντρο της πόλης; (How do I get to the city center?)

3. Πού είναι το πλησιέστερο φαρμακείο; (Where is the nearest pharmacy?)

Practicing these phrases will help you feel more confident and prepared when asking for directions in Greek.

By equipping yourself with these phrases, you'll find it much easier to navigate, ask for help, and seek information during your time in Greece. These skills make your experiences smoother and show your willingness to engage with and understand the local culture. Regular practice will make these phrases second nature, allowing you to communicate more effectively and enjoy your time in Greece.

4.3 Making Small Talk

Small talk is an art that makes social interactions smoother and more enjoyable. Knowing how to discuss the weather can be a great icebreaker. When you want to ask about the weather, you can use the phrase, "Τι καιρό κάνει σήμερα;" (What is the weather like today?). This is a great way to start a conversation, especially with someone you've just met. If the weather is particularly notable, you can say, "Είναι πολύ ζεστό έξω" (It is very hot outside) or "Είναι πολύ κρύο έξω" (It is very cold outside). These phrases are simple yet effective for initiating a friendly chat.

Discussing hobbies and interests is another excellent way to connect with others. You might ask, "Ασχολείσαι με κάποιο χόμπι;" (Do you have any hobbies?). This question opens up a dialogue about personal interests and activities. If you're sharing your hobbies, you can say, "Μου αρέσει να διαβάζω βιβλία" (I like reading books) or "Παίζω κιθάρα" (I play the guitar). These statements provide a glimpse into your personal life and can lead to more engaging conversations. Sharing hobbies is a great way to find common ground and build rapport.

Current events are often on people's minds and can be an engaging topic of conversation. You might ask, "Άκουσες τι έγινε στις ειδήσεις σήμερα;" (Did you hear what happened in the news today?). This question can lead to a discussion about recent events and news stories. If you're interested in someone's opinion on a particular issue, you might ask, "Τι γνώμη έχεις για την πολιτική κατάσταση;" (What do you think about the political situation?). These questions show you're informed and interested in current affairs, making the conversation more meaningful.

Daily life is a topic everyone can relate to and is perfect for making small talk. Asking about someone's work is an excellent place to start. You might say, "Πού δουλεύεις;" (Where do you work?). This question can lead to a discussion about their job and daily activities. If you want to know how someone's day has been, you can ask, "Πώς ήταν η μέρα σου;" (How was your day?). This straightforward question shows genuine interest in the other person's well-being. Finally, discussing weekend plans is a great way to wrap up the week. You can ask, "Τι σχέδια έχεις για το Σαββατοκύριακο;" (What plans do you have for the weekend?). This question can lead to a fun, light-hearted conversation about leisure activities and upcoming events.

Small talk may seem trivial, but it builds connections and makes social interactions more enjoyable. Whether you're discussing the weather, hobbies, current events, or daily life, these topics provide a foundation for more meaningful conversations. By practicing these phrases, you'll become more comfortable engaging in small talk, making your interactions in Greek more natural and enjoyable.

4.4 Expressing Preferences and Opinions

Expressing what you like and dislike can make conversations more exciting and personal. Imagine you're at a Greek taverna and want to share your love for Greek food. You might say, "Μου αρέσει..." (I like...), followed by the dish you enjoy. For instance, "Μου αρέσει ο μουσακάς" (I like moussaka). On the flip side, if there's something you're not fond of, you can say, "Δεν μου αρέσει..." (I don't like...). For example, "Δεν μου αρέσουν οι ελιές" (I don't like olives). These phrases are simple yet powerful for expressing your tastes and preferences. If you have a strong preference for something, "Προτιμώ..." (I prefer...) is the phrase to use. For instance, "Προτιμώ τον καφέ από το τσάι" (I prefer coffee to tea). These expressions help you communicate your likes and dislikes clearly and effectively.

Giving your opinion is another important aspect of communication. Whether discussing a book, a movie, or a political issue, knowing how to express your thoughts can lead to engaging conversations. You might start with "Νομίζω ότι..." (I think that...), which is a neutral way to share your opinion. For example, "Νομίζω ότι αυτή η ταινία είναι καλή" (I think that this movie is good). If you want to emphasize that it's your personal view, you can say, "Κατά τη γνώμη μου..." (In my opinion...). For instance, "Κατά τη γνώμη μου, αυτό το βιβλίο είναι ενδιαφέρον" (In my opinion, this book is interesting). Agreeing or disagreeing with someone is also a crucial part of conversations. You can say, "Συμφωνώ" (I agree) or "Διαφωνώ" (I disagree). These phrases are essential for expressing your stance on various topics.

Comparing options is a standard part of everyday conversations. Whether you're choosing a restaurant, a travel destination, or even a movie to watch, knowing how to compare can help you communicate your preferences. You might say, "Αυτό είναι καλύτερο από..." (This is better than...), to express that you prefer one thing over another. For example, "Αυτό το εστιατόριο είναι καλύτερο από το άλλο" (This restaurant is better than the other one). If you have a strong preference, you can use "Προτιμώ αυτό παρά..." (I prefer this over...). For instance, "Προτιμώ την παραλία παρά το βουνό" (I prefer the beach over the mountains). These phrases help make comparisons and express your choices.

Asking for someone else's opinion shows that you're interested in their thoughts and can lead to more engaging conversations. You might ask, "Τι γνώμη έχεις για αυτό;" (What do you think about this?). This open-ended question invites the other person to share their views. If you're curious if they like something, "Σου αρέσει αυτό;" (Do you like this?) is a straightforward way to ask. For instance, "Σου αρέσει αυτό το τραγούδι;" (Do you like this song?). To get a more emotional response, you can ask, "Πώς νιώθεις για αυτό;" (How do you feel about this?). This question digs deeper into their feelings and can lead to a richer conversation.

By mastering these phrases for expressing preferences and opinions, you'll find it easier to communicate your likes, dislikes, and thoughts on various topics. These expressions are fundamental for engaging in meaningful conversations and building connections. Whether you share your love for Greek cuisine, discuss a recent movie, or compare travel destinations, these phrases will help you express yourself clearly and confidently. Keep practicing, and soon, you'll find these expressions becoming a natural part of your conversations in Greek.

4.5 Talking About Daily Activities

Discussing your daily activities in Greek can help you connect with others and share a bit about your life. Starting with your morning routine is an excellent way to begin these conversations. You might say, "Ξυπνάω στις..." (I wake up at...), followed by when you usually wake up. For instance, "Ξυπνάω στις επτά" (I wake up at seven). This simple phrase sets the stage for sharing more about your morning. After waking up, you might have breakfast, which you can describe with the phrase, "Παίρνω πρωινό στις..." (I have breakfast at...). For example, "Παίρνω πρωινό στις οχτώ" (I have breakfast at eight). If you're heading to work, you can say, "Πηγαίνω στη δουλειά με..." (I go to work by...), followed by your mode of transportation. For instance, "Πηγαίνω στη δουλειά με το λεωφορείο" (I go to work by bus). These phrases give a clear picture of your morning routine and make for engaging conversation starters.

Talking about work and school involves critical phrases applicable to everyday conversations. If you want to share your work schedule, you might say, "Δουλεύω από τις... μέχρι τις..." (I work from... to...). For example, "Δουλεύω από τις εννέα μέχρι τις πέντε" (I work from nine to five). This phrase helps others understand your daily routine. If you're a student, you might say, "Πηγαίνω στο σχολείο στις..." (I go to school at...), such as "Πηγαίνω στο σχολείο στις οχτώ" (I go to school at eight). When talking about your evening, you can mention when you return home with the phrase, "Επιστρέφω σπίτι στις..." (I return home at...). For example, "Επιστρέφω σπίτι στις έξι" (I return home at six). These phrases are essential for discussing your daily schedule and making plans with others.

Evening activities often include dinner and relaxation. To talk about when you have dinner, you can use the phrase, "Δειπνώ στις..." (I have dinner at...), such as "Δειπνώ στις επτά" (I have dinner at seven). After dinner, you might want to relax by watching TV. You can say, "Παρακολουθώ τηλεόραση" (I watch TV). This simple phrase can lead to conversations about your favorite shows or movies. When it's time to go to bed, you can say, "Πηγαίνω για ύπνο στις..." (I go to bed at...), such as "Πηγαίνω για ύπνο στις δέκα" (I go to bed at ten). These phrases help you share your evening routine and can lead to more in-depth conversations about your daily life.

Discussing weekend plans in Greek can make your conversations more engaging and help you connect with others. You might start by asking, "Τι κάνεις συνήθως το Σαββατοκύριακο;" (What do you usually do on weekends?). This question opens up a dialogue about weekend activities. If you plan to go shopping, you can say, "Θα πάω για ψώνια" (I will go shopping). This phrase helps you share your plans and can lead to discussions about your favorite shopping spots. If you plan to meet friends, you can say, "Θα συναντήσω φίλους" (I will meet friends). This phrase can lead to conversations about social activities and favorite hangout spots.

Using these phrases to discuss your daily activities can help you share more about your life and learn about others. Whether discussing your morning routine, work schedule, evening activities, or weekend plans, these phrases help you connect with others and make your conversations more meaningful. Keep practicing these expressions, and you'll find yourself more comfortable discussing your daily life in Greek, making your interactions richer and more enjoyable.

4.6 Making Plans and Arrangements

Setting appointments in Greek is crucial for social and professional interactions. Imagine you want to meet a friend for coffee. You can ask, "Μπορούμε να συναντηθούμε στις..." (Can we meet at...), followed by the time. For example, "Μπορούμε να συναντηθούμε στις τρεις;" (Can we meet at three?). This phrase is flexible and can be used for various times and settings. If you already have an appointment and want to share this information, you can say, "Έχω ραντεβού στις..." (I have an appointment at...). For instance, "Έχω ραντεβού στις δύο" (I have an appointment at two). This is useful for planning around existing commitments. To find out someone's availability, you might ask, "Πότε είσαι ελεύθερος;" (When are you free?). This question helps you coordinate schedules and set a convenient time for both parties.

Inviting someone to an event or activity is a beautiful way to build connections. Suppose you ask a friend to join you for a fun outing. You can say, "Θέλεις να έρθεις μαζί μας;" (Do you want to come with us?). This phrase is casual and perfect for friendly invitations. If you're hosting a celebration, such as a birthday party, you might use "Σε προσκαλώ στο πάρτι μου" (I invite you to my party). This formal invitation shows thoughtfulness and effort, making the invitee feel special. For a more relaxed setting, like grabbing coffee, you can ask, "Θα ήθελες να πάμε για καφέ;" (Would you like to go for a coffee?). These phrases are versatile and can be tailored to various events and activities, helping you extend invitations warmly and clearly.

Confirming plans is essential to ensure everyone is on the same page. If you've made plans for the next day and want to check if they're still on, you can ask, "Είμαστε ακόμα για αύριο το βράδυ;" (Are we still on for tomorrow night?). This phrase is straightforward and helps avoid any last-minute confusion. When the other person confirms, they might say, "Ναι, θα είμαι εκεί" (Yes, I will be there). This confirmation reassures you that the plan is set. However, sometimes plans change, and you might need to cancel. In such cases, you can say, "Δυστυχώς, πρέπει να ακυρώσω" (Unfortunately, I have to cancel). This polite phrase shows that you value the other person's time, even though you must change the plans.

Adjusting plans is sometimes necessary, and knowing how to do this politely is essential. If you need to adjust the timing of a meeting, you can ask, "Μπορούμε να αλλάξουμε την ώρα;" (Can we change the time?). This respectful question opens up a dialogue for finding a new time that works for everyone. If rescheduling to a different day is required, you might say, "Θα ήθελα να το μεταθέσουμε για άλλη μέρα"

(I would like to reschedule for another day). This phrase is clear and considerate, showing that you still want to meet but need a different date. To find out the other person's availability, you can ask, "Ποια άλλη μέρα σε βολεύει;" (What other day works for you?). This helps you find a mutually convenient time for rescheduling.

By mastering these phrases for setting appointments, inviting others, confirming plans, and making changes, you'll find it easier to organize and manage your social and professional life. These skills are invaluable for maintaining clear and respectful communication ensuring that plans run smoothly and everyone is on the same page. Keep practicing these phrases to become more confident and efficient in making arrangements in Greek.

Review Page

Make a Difference with Your Review
Unlock the Power of Generosity

"One of the greatest joys in life is helping others." - Anonymous

When you give without expecting anything in return, you help make the world a better place. Now, let's make a difference together!

Are you curious about learning Greek but unsure where to begin? If you've found **The Complete Beginner's Guide to Learning Greek** by **M. J. Perreault** helpful, your experience could guide someone else's language journey.

My goal is to make learning Greek *easy and fun* for everyone.

But I need your help to reach more people just starting out like you once were. Most readers decide which books to choose based on reviews from other readers. By leaving a review, you could help someone else take that important first step toward learning Greek.

It costs nothing and takes less than a minute, but your review could make a huge difference for someone eager to learn. Your words might help...

...a student gets excited about mastering a new language.
...a traveler confidently speaks Greek on their next adventure.
...someone fulfills their dream of learning a new skill.

To help, simply scan the QR code below and leave a review:
[https://www.amazon.com/review/review-your-purchases/?asin=B0
DKCDBMDX]

If you enjoy helping others, you're my kind of person. Thank you
so much for supporting this mission and joining this journey!

M. J. Perreault

Chapter 5: Pronunciation and Listening Practice

This chapter focuses on helping you avoid common pronunciation mistakes and provides strategies to strengthen your skills.

5.1 Common Pronunciation Mistakes and How to Avoid Them

One of the most common mistakes beginners make is mispronouncing Greek diphthongs. Greek has several diphthongs like "οι", "ει", "αι", "ευ", and "αυ". These are pairs of vowels pronounced as a single sound. For example, "οι" and "ει" both sound like "i" as in "info," while "αι" sounds like "e" in "error." The diphthong "ευ" can sound like "ev" in "everything" or "ef" in "effect" depending on the following syllable, and "αυ" can sound like "av" in "average" or "af" in "after." Getting these sounds wrong can lead to misunderstandings. For instance, the word "καὶ" (and) pronounced correctly sounds like "ke," but if you mispronounce it, it could confuse the listener.

Another frequent issue is clarification on similar-sounding consonants. Greek has sounds that may seem subtle to non-native speakers but are crucial for clarity. Take β (beta) and φ (phi), for example. B sounds like the "v" in "victory," while φ sounds like "f" in "fun." Mixing these up can lead to confusion. Similarly, τ (tau) and δ (delta) can be tricky. T sounds like the "t" in "top," while δ is similar to the "th" in "this." Mispronouncing these can entirely change the meaning of a word. For example, "τάξη" (class) and "δάση" (forests) are two distinct words that can be easily confused if mispronounced.

Incorrect stress placement is another common mistake. Unlike English, where stress can vary, Greek has specific stress rules. Each Greek word has one stressed syllable, and misplacing it can alter its meaning. For instance, "πόνος" (pain) with stress on the first syllable is different from "πονώ" (I hurt) with stress on the second. Beginners often stress words incorrectly, leading to confusion. Understanding where to place the stress is vital for clear communication. Resources like GreekPod101 emphasize the importance of stress in their lessons, helping learners practice correct stress placement.

To avoid these common mistakes, practice with minimal pairs—words that differ by only one sound. For example, practice saying "πίτα" (pie) and "πύτα" (putty) to distinguish vowel sounds. Minimal pairs can help you fine-tune your ear and mouth to the subtleties of Greek pronunciation. Mnemonic devices can also be helpful. For instance, to remember that "ευ" can sound like "ef" or "ev," associate it with English words like "effect" and "everything." These small tricks can make a big difference in mastering pronunciation.

Correcting pronunciation errors involves several strategies. One effective method is recording and listening to your pronunciation. This allows you to hear your mistakes and work on them. Comparing your pronunciation with native speaker audio clips provides a benchmark for improvement. Many language learning platforms, like GreekPod101, offer voice-recording tools to compare your pronunciation with native speakers. Another valuable approach is seeking feedback from native speakers or teachers. They can provide insights and corrections you might need to look alone. Personalized guidance can significantly accelerate your learning process.

Practice exercises are essential for reinforcing correct pronunciation. Start with repetition drills for troublesome sounds. For example, if you struggle with the diphthong "ευ," practice words like "ευχαριστώ" (thank you). Sentence-level practice with a focus on stress placement is also beneficial. Try reading sentences aloud, paying attention to where the stress falls. Audio resources can guide you through this process. Websites like GreekPod101 offer slowed-down audio clips to help you catch every nuance. Regular practice will make these sounds and stress patterns second nature.

You can significantly improve your Greek pronunciation by focusing on these common mistakes and using the strategies provided. Remember, practice and persistence are key. Each small step brings you closer to sounding like a native speaker.

5.2 Listening to Native Speakers

Listening to native speakers is a crucial part of learning Greek. It exposes you to the natural flow of the language, allowing you to hear how words and phrases are used in everyday conversations. This exposure helps you understand intonation and rhythm, which are essential for sounding natural when speaking. You'll notice patterns in how sentences rise and fall, how questions are asked, and how emphasis is placed on certain words. It's not just about hearing the words; it's about understanding the musicality of the language. Listening also familiarizes you with colloquial expressions and slang, which textbooks often overlook. These elements of spoken Greek are vital for real-life interactions.

Finding quality listening resources is the next step. Greek radio stations and podcasts are excellent starting points. They offer a wide range of content, from news to entertainment, and expose you to different accents and dialects. Websites like GreekPod101 provide structured lessons that include audio clips of native speakers. These resources are designed to help you start speaking Greek from the first lesson. Online streaming platforms offer access to Greek TV shows and movies, which are fantastic for hearing conversational Greek in various contexts. Watching shows with subtitles can help you match spoken words with their written forms, reinforcing your learning.

Active listening techniques can significantly enhance your comprehension skills. Start by taking notes while you listen. Write down unfamiliar words and phrases, then look them up later. This practice helps you focus and retain new information. Identifying keywords and phrases is another effective technique. Pay attention to repeated words and common expressions. These are often crucial for understanding the main idea of the conversation. Summarizing what you've heard in your own words can also be helpful. After listening to a podcast or watching a show, try to summarize the content. This exercise forces you to process and internalize what you've heard, improving your comprehension.

Listening comprehension exercises can further refine your skills. Start with comprehension questions based on audio clips. For example, listen to a short dialogue and answer questions about it. This will test your understanding and help you focus on crucial details. Transcription exercises are another valuable tool. Listen to a sentence or short passage and write down what you hear. This practice improves your ability to catch every word and understand the flow of the language. Listening and repeating dialogues can also be very effective. Find dialogues that interest you, listen to them several times, and then try to repeat them. This exercise helps you practice pronunciation and intonation while reinforcing your listening skills.

Interactive Exercise: Listening Comprehension Practice

Listen to a short audio clip from a Greek radio station or podcast. Write down the main points and any new words you hear. Try to answer the following questions:

1. What is the main topic of the audio clip?

2. Who are the speakers, and what are their roles?

3. What new words did you learn, and what do they mean?

These exercises and techniques will help you become a more effective listener, enabling you to understand and engage in conversations with native Greek speakers more confidently.

5.3 Mimicking Native Pronunciation

One of the most effective techniques for improving your Greek pronunciation is shadowing. The shadowing technique involves listening to a native speaker and repeating what they say immediately, trying to mimic their pronunciation as closely as possible. This method helps you internalize the language's sounds, rhythm, and intonation. Shadowing is beneficial because it forces you to pay close attention to how words are pronounced and to practice speaking them in real-time. It's like having a personal tutor you can imitate, honing your fluency and pronunciation skills with each repetition.

To practice shadowing, start by selecting appropriate material. Short dialogues or monologues are ideal for beginners. These shorter segments allow you to focus on specific phrases without feeling overwhelmed. Slow-speed recordings are also beneficial as they give you more time to catch each word and sound. Audio clips with clear pronunciation are essential; you must hear each word distinctly to mimic it accurately. GreekPod101 offers a treasure trove of such materials, with lessons designed to help you start speaking Greek from the first lesson. The key is to choose content that matches your current level and gradually increases in complexity.

Structuring your practice sessions effectively is crucial for getting the most out of shadowing. Begin with short segments of a few seconds. Listen to the native speaker, then immediately repeat what you heard. Focus on intonation and rhythm, matching the speaker's tone and pace. Gradually increase the length of the segments as you become more comfortable. Recording your practice sessions can be beneficial. Listen to the recordings to identify areas where you deviate from the native speaker and adjust as needed. This iterative listening, repeating, and reviewing process helps refine your pronunciation.

Common challenges can arise when practicing shadowing, but there are strategies to overcome them. One issue is difficulty keeping up with native speakers. If you find this challenging, use slow-speed recordings or slow down the audio yourself. Repeat the segments multiple times until you can keep pace with the speaker. Another common problem is mispronouncing certain sounds. Focus on these sounds individually, practicing them in isolation before incorporating them into complete sentences. For example, if you struggle with the diphthong "ευ," isolate it and practice it in different words before including it in sentences. Consistent practice and attention to detail will help you overcome these challenges.

By incorporating shadowing into your daily practice, your pronunciation improves steadily. Each session brings you closer to speaking Greek with the fluency and naturalness of a native speaker.

5.4 Phonetic Transcription Exercises

When I first encountered the International Phonetic Alphabet (IPA), it felt like deciphering a secret code. Yet, learning IPA can significantly improve your pronunciation. IPA is a system of symbols representing each sound in a language. For Greek, these symbols help you understand how to pronounce words accurately. For instance, the Greek letter "θ" is transcribed as [θ], similar to the "th" sound in "think." The symbol [i] represents the "ee" sound in "see," and [o] describes the "o" sound in "go." Learning these symbols can make a world of difference in your pronunciation.

The benefits of learning IPA are numerous:

1. It provides a clear and consistent way to understand pronunciation, free from the irregularities of traditional spelling. This consistency is beneficial for Greek, where letters like "ο" and "ω" both make the same "o" sound.

2. IPA allows you to read pronunciation guides in dictionaries and language resources accurately.

3. It helps you develop a more native-like accent by focusing on the actual sounds of the language rather than just the letters.

Let's look at some examples to begin transcribing common Greek words using IPA. The word "νερό" (water) is transcribed as [neˈro], with the stress on the second syllable. Another example is "καλημέρα" (good morning), which is transcribed as [ka.liˈme.ra], with the stress on the penultimate syllable—practice by transcribing a list of common words. For example, try transcribing "σπίτι" (house) and "αγάπη" (love). Write down your transcriptions and check them against a reliable IPA chart or language resource.

Listening and transcribing exercises are an effective way to reinforce your learning. Start by listening to audio clips of individual words or short sentences. Write down what you hear using IPA symbols. For instance, listen to the word "καφές" (coffee) and transcribe it as [kaˈfes]. This practice sharpens your listening skills and helps you connect sounds with their IPA symbols. Allocate space in your notebook to write your transcriptions, and try to be as accurate as possible. This exercise will help you internalize the sounds of Greek.

After completing your transcriptions:

1. Review your work with an answer key.

2. Compare your transcriptions to the correct ones provided.

3. Consider common errors, such as misplacing stress marks or confusing similar sounds.

For example, you might mistakenly transcribe "γιαγιά" (grand-mother) as [ˈja.ja] instead of the correct [jaˈja]. Understanding these mistakes will help you improve. Tips for correction include focusing on placing stress marks and practicing troublesome sounds separately.

Answer Key and Tips for Correction

Examples of correct transcriptions:

1. νερό (water) - [neˈro]

2. καλημέρα (good morning) - [ka.liˈme.ra]

3. σπίτι (house) - [ˈspi.ti]

4. αγάπη (love) - [aˈɣa.pi]

Common errors and tips:

1. Incorrect stress placement: Ensure you place stress marks on the correct syllable.

2. Confusing similar sounds: Listen to native speakers and practice distinguishing sounds like [θ] and [ð].

Use these exercises and tips to refine your phonetic transcription skills. By incorporating IPA into your practice, you'll find that your pronunciation becomes more accurate and natural. Consistent practice with these techniques will help you become more confident in understanding and speaking Greek.

5.5 Tongue Twisters for Pronunciation Practice

When I started practicing Greek tongue twisters, I found them challenging and incredibly fun. They are a fantastic way to improve pronunciation and fluency. Tongue twisters force you to practice challenging sounds, repeatedly enhancing your articulation and speed. Imagine trying to say "Πέντε παπάκια πήγανε στην ποταμιά" (Five little ducks went to the river) quickly. It's a workout for your mouth! Beyond the physical practice, tongue twisters engage your brain, making learning more interactive and enjoyable. They add an element of fun to what can sometimes be a tedious process, keeping you motivated.

Let's look at some popular Greek tongue twisters. One of my favorites is "Πέντε παπάκια πήγανε στην ποταμιά." This phrase is great for practicing Greek sentences' "π" sound and rhythm. Another classic is "Σαράντα σαράντα σαράντα σαρδέλες" (Forty forty forty sardines), which focuses on the "σ" sound. It's a bit of a tongue-twister even for native speakers, making it a perfect challenge for learners. Lastly, there's "Καθόταν η καλή καλή καλαμαράκι" (The good good squid was sitting), which helps with practicing the "κ" sound in various positions within words. These tongue twisters are entertaining and practical tools for improving your pronunciation.

Practicing tongue twisters effectively requires a few techniques. Start slowly to ensure you're pronouncing each word. Speed will come with practice. Focus on clear articulation, making sure each sound is distinct. For example, when saying "Πέντε παπάκια πήγανε στην ποταμιά," ensure each "π" sound is crisp. Gradually increase your speed as you become more comfortable. Repeating the tongue twister multiple times helps build muscle memory and fluency. It's like training for a marathon—start slow, build up your endurance, and increase your speed.

Learners often face common challenges with tongue twisters, such as tripping over words or struggling with specific sounds. If you find yourself stumbling, break the tongue twister into smaller parts. Practice each segment slowly, then gradually put them together. For instance, if "Σαράντα σαράντα σαράντα σαρδέλες" is tricky, start with "Σαράντα" and then add "σαράντα σαρδέλες" once you're comfortable. Another strategy is to isolate and practice complex sounds individually before integrating them into the tongue twister. This method helps you build confidence and precision.

5.6 Using Audio Resources Effectively

Finding quality audio resources can be a game-changer in your Greek learning experience. Language learning apps with native speaker recordings are a fantastic starting point. These apps provide clear, consistent examples of how native speakers speak Greek. Websites like GreekPod101 offer thousands of audio and video lessons to help you understand honest Greek conversations. Another excellent source is online platforms for Greek radio, podcasts, and audiobooks. These resources expose you to various accents and dialects, helping you get used to the natural flow of the language. Educational websites with audio content tailored for learners also provide valuable practice. These sites often break down complex sentences into manageable parts and offer slowed-down audio to help you catch every nuance.

Integrating audio into your daily practice can make a significant difference. One effective method is to listen during your commutes or while doing chores. This passive exposure allows you to absorb the sounds of Greek without requiring focused attention. Setting aside dedicated time for focused listening is also crucial. During these sessions, pay close attention to pronunciation, intonation, and stress patterns. Combining audio with other learning activities can enhance your understanding. For example, reading along with transcripts while listening to audio can help reinforce what you hear and see. This dual approach solidifies your comprehension and pronunciation skills.

Understanding the difference between active and passive listening is essential for effective practice. Active listening involves techniques like note-taking and summarizing, which engage you more deeply with the content. For instance, while listening to a Greek podcast, jot down unfamiliar words and phrases, then look them up later. This method helps you focus and retain new information. On the other hand, passive listening involves having Greek audio in the background while you go about your day. This technique exposes you to the language more relaxedly, helping you absorb it naturally. Both types of listening have their benefits, and balancing them can significantly enhance your learning experience.

Tracking your progress is critical to staying motivated and seeing tangible improvements. Keeping a listening journal is a simple yet effective method. Note new words, phrases, and expressions you encounter during your listening sessions. This practice helps you track what you've learned and identify areas that need more attention. Recording and reviewing your pronunciation can also be highly beneficial. Listen to your recordings and compare them with native speakers. This exercise helps you pinpoint areas for improvement and track your progress over time. Regular self-assessment quizzes measure your progress, highlighting strengths and areas that need more focus. These methods ensure you stay motivated and on track with your learning goals.

Incorporating these strategies into your daily routine can significantly improve your ability to understand and speak Greek. By utilizing high-quality audio resources, integrating them into your practice, understanding the benefits of active and passive listening, and tracking your progress, you'll become more confident and proficient in Greek. Each step you take brings you closer to fluency, making your Greek learning experience more rewarding and enjoyable.

Chapter 6:
Cultural Context
and Insights

This chapter aims to give you an insightful look into the customs and traditions integral to Greek daily life. By understanding these, you'll navigate social situations better and appreciate the rich cultural tapestry that makes Greece unique.

6.1 Greek Customs and Traditions

Greek customs are deeply woven into the fabric of daily life, influencing everything from social interactions to festive celebrations. One of the first things you'll notice is how Greeks greet each other. Traditional Greek greetings often involve a kiss on both cheeks, especially among friends and family. This gesture may seem intimate to those unfamiliar, but it is a common way to express warmth and affection. In more formal settings, a handshake is appropriate. The importance of family and community gatherings cannot be overstated in Greek culture.

Family units are close-knit, and it's common for extended families to live near each other or gather frequently for meals and celebrations. Community gatherings, whether for religious festivals or local events, foster a strong sense of belonging and mutual support.

Religion plays a significant role in Greek customs, with the Greek Orthodox Church being a central pillar of cultural life. Approximately 98% of Greeks identify as Christian Orthodox, and the church's influence is evident in many aspects of daily life. Religious practices and holidays are observed with great reverence. Easter, known as "Πάσχα," is the most important religious celebration in Greece. The week leading up to Easter Sunday is filled with various rituals, including the Good Friday procession and the midnight Resurrection service on Saturday, where people gather in churches holding lit candles. The greeting "Χριστός Ανέστη!" (Christ is Risen!) is exchanged, followed by a response of "Αληθώς Ανέστη!" (Truly, He is Risen!). These traditions are religious observances and times for family and community bonding.

Festive traditions in Greece are rich and varied, offering a glimpse into the country's unique cultural heritage. Name-day celebrations often take precedence over birthdays. Each day of the year is dedicated to the memory of a saint, and people named after that saint celebrate their "name day." It's common for friends and family to visit, bringing small gifts or sweets. Traditional Greek weddings are another fascinating aspect of Greek culture. These ceremonies are elaborate and filled with rituals that symbolize the union of the couple and the blessing of their families. The exchange of rings, the crowning ceremony, and the dance of Isaiah are just a few elements that make Greek weddings memorable and meaningful.

Cultural symbols in Greece carry deep significance and are often seen in everyday life. The evil eye, or "μάτι," is a familiar protective charm believed to ward off negative energy and jealousy. You'll see these blue eye-shaped amulets in homes, cars, and even as jewelry. Another significant symbol is the Greek flag, which embodies the country's rich history and national pride. The blue and white flag represents the sea and the waves, and the cross signifies the Greek Orthodox faith. The national anthem, "Ύμνος εις την Ελευθερίαν" (Hymn to Liberty), further evokes the spirit of freedom and resilience that characterizes the Greek people.

Understanding these customs and traditions will not only help you navigate social interactions in Greece but also allow you to appreciate the depth and richness of Greek culture. Whether you participate in a festive celebration, attend a religious service, or share a meal with a local family, these insights will enrich your experience and deepen your connection to this vibrant country.

Reflection Section: Your Greek Cultural Experience

Take a few moments to reflect on what you've learned about Greek customs and traditions. How do these compare to customs and traditions in your own culture? Write down a few thoughts or experiences you've had while exploring Greek culture. This reflection will help you internalize what you've learned and prepare you for more meaningful interactions during your time in Greece.

6.2 Cultural Etiquette and Social Norms

Greeting etiquette in Greece is nuanced and can vary depending on the level of familiarity and the context. In formal settings, a firm handshake is customary and conveys respect. When addressing someone older or in a position of authority, it's polite to use their title and last name. For example, "κύριε Παπαδόπουλε" (Mr. Papadopoulos) or "κυρία Καραγιάννη" (Mrs. Karagianni). Greetings are warmer and more personal in informal situations, especially among friends and family. Hugs and cheek kisses are common. Typically, Greeks kiss each other on both cheeks, starting with the right. This gesture is a sign of affection and familiarity. It's also important to show respect to elders by standing when they enter a room and addressing them with honorifics. These gestures reflect the high value Greeks place on respect and interpersonal relationships.

Dining etiquette in Greece is a blend of formality and warmth. When invited to a Greek home for a meal, bringing a small gift, such as wine, sweets, or flowers, is customary. This gesture shows appreciation and respect for the host's hospitality. Waiting for the host to invite you to start eating is polite at the table. Greeks have a tradition of passing food to the left, and it's common for everyone to share dishes, especially in informal settings. Bread is usually served without butter and is often used to soak up sauces and gravies. Keep your hands visible above the table, resting your wrists on the edge when not using utensils. After the meal, crossing your knife and fork on your plate with the knife underneath and the fork tines facing down indicates that you have finished eating. Hospitality is a cornerstone of Greek culture, and guests are treated with great care. Accepting food and drink graciously and complimenting the host on the meal are ways to show appreciation.

Social norms in Greece are deeply rooted in tradition and community values. Punctuality is more relaxed compared to some other cultures. It's common for social gatherings to start a bit later than the scheduled time. However, for business meetings, punctuality is expected. Personal space in Greece is also more intimate. Greeks tend to stand closer to each other during conversations, and physical contact, such as a pat on the back or a touch on the arm, is common. These gestures are signs of friendliness and trust. Gift-giving is an essential social custom. When visiting someone's home, bringing a gift is a thoughtful gesture. Small items like sweets, wine, or flowers are appreciated. When giving and receiving gifts, it's polite to do so with both hands and opening the gift in front of the giver is customary to show appreciation.

Professional etiquette in Greece is a blend of formality and personal connection. Dressing appropriately is essential in business settings. Men wear suits and ties, while women opt for conservative business attire. Business meetings often begin with small talk to build rapport before moving on to the main agenda. Discussing personal topics such as family or mutual acquaintances is expected to establish trust. When exchanging business cards, do so with both hands and take a moment to read the card before putting it away. This gesture shows respect and interest. Greeks value building personal relationships in business and getting to know your colleagues or business partners can enhance your professional interactions.

Understanding these aspects of Greek cultural etiquette and social norms will help you quickly navigate various social and professional settings. Whether you are greeting someone, dining with friends, or attending a business meeting, these insights will guide you in showing respect and building meaningful connections.

6.3 Important Greek Holidays and Festivals

Greece is a land of vibrant traditions, and its national holidays are among the most significant events that unite communities. Independence Day is one of the most important national holidays, celebrated on March 25th. This day commemorates Greece's independence from Ottoman rule in 1821. The country comes alive with parades, patriotic songs, and traditional dances. Military parades featuring soldiers in conventional Greek uniforms are central to the celebrations. People gather in public squares, waving Greek flags and enjoying the festive atmosphere. Schools, government offices, and businesses close for the day, allowing everyone to participate in the festivities.

Another significant national holiday is Ohi Day, observed on October 28th. This day marks Greece's defiance against the Italian ultimatum during World War II. "Ohi" means "No," symbolizing the refusal to surrender. Like Independence Day, Ohi Day is celebrated with military and student parades and public speeches. It's a day of national pride, and the streets are filled with people waving flags and cheering. The bravery and resilience of the Greek people during the war are remembered and honored. Schools and businesses close, allowing everyone to take part in the celebrations.

Religious festivals are unique in Greek culture, with Easter being the most significant. Greek Easter, or "Πάσχα," is celebrated with various customs and rituals that bring communities together. One of the most memorable customs is the midnight mass on Holy Saturday, where people gather in churches holding lit candles. As the clock strikes midnight, the priest announces, "Χριστός Ανέστη!" (Christ is Risen!), and the congregation responds, "Αληθώς Ανέστη!" (Truly, He is Risen!). The celebratory atmosphere continues with fireworks and the traditional cracking of red-dyed eggs, symbolizing the resurrection. Easter Sunday is marked by feasting on roasted lamb and various festive dishes, bringing families together for a joyful celebration.

Christmas in Greece is another deeply cherished holiday, observed with unique traditions. Caroling, known as "κάλαντα," is a beloved activity where children go from house to house singing Christmas songs and receiving small treats or money in re-

bakif Chrissomo

turn. Christmas Eve is a time for families to gather and enjoy a festive meal. One particular tradition is the bakif Chrissomo, or "Christ's bread," sweet bread decorated with a cross and other symbols. This bread is often shared with family and friends, symbolizing unity and blessings for the coming year. The holiday season extends to New Year's Day, celebrated with the cutting of the Vassilopita, a cake with a hidden coin that brings good luck to the finder.

Cultural festivals are integral to Greek life, offering a rich music, theater, and dance tapestry. The Athens and Epidaurus Festival is one of the most notable events, attracting artists and audiences worldwide. Held in ancient theaters like the Odeon of Herodes Atticus and the Epidaurus

Vassilopita

Theater, the festival features various performances, including classical plays, contemporary theater, and musical concerts. These performances are a mesmerizing blend of ancient and modern, offering a unique cultural experience.

The Thessaloniki International Film Festival is another significant event celebrating Greek and international cinema. Held annually in the vibrant city of Thessaloniki, the festival showcases various films, from independent productions to major releases. It's a platform for filmmakers to present their work and for audiences to explore new cinematic horizons. The festival includes film screenings, workshops, and discussions, making it a dynamic and engaging event for film enthusiasts.

Local traditions and festivals add another layer of richness to Greek cultural life. Carnival, or "Apokries," is a lively celebration that takes place before the start of Lent. Parades, masquerades, and various festivities mark it. Cities like Patras are renowned for their grand carnival parades, where people dress in elaborate costumes, dance, and celebrate in the streets. Village festivals, known as "panigiria," honor patron saints and are celebrated with traditional music, dancing, and feasting. These festivals are deeply rooted in local customs and allow communities to unite and celebrate their shared heritage.

6.4 Greek Cuisine and Dining Etiquette

Greek cuisine is a delightful blend of flavors, textures, and aromas deeply rooted in the country's history and geography. At the heart of Greek cooking are simple, fresh ingredients that create rich, flavorful dishes. Olive oil is a staple in almost every Greek dish, lending a smooth, rich taste to salads, dips, and cooked meals. Herbs such as oregano, thyme, and rosemary are used generously, often picked fresh from the countryside. Feta cheese, with its crumbly texture and tangy flavor, accompanies many meals, from salads to pies. These ingredients are not just add-ons but essential components that define the essence of Greek cuisine.

Popular dishes in Greece are a testament to the country's culinary heritage. Moussaka, a layered dish made with eggplant, minced meat, and béchamel sauce, is a favorite in many households. Souvlaki, skewers of grilled meat often served with pita bread and tzatziki, is a beloved street food. Tzatziki, a refreshing dip made from yogurt, cucumber, and garlic, perfectly accompanies many meals. These dishes reflect the Greek love for hearty, flavorful food that brings people together. Whether trying a traditional dish at a local taverna or making it at home, these flavors will leave a lasting impression.

The structure of Greek meals typically starts with mezze, small appetizers that are perfect for sharing. These can include dishes like dolmades (stuffed grape leaves), spanakopita (spinach pie), and olives. Mezze sets the stage for the main course, which often features grilled meats, fresh fish, or hearty stews. Side dishes like horta (boiled greens) and fava (split pea purée) complement the main course. Desserts and sweets are an essential part of the meal, with treats like baklava, a sweet pastry made with layers of filo dough, nuts, and honey syrup, or loukoumades, small honey-soaked donuts. This multi-course structure encourages leisurely dining, allowing time for conversation and connection.

Dining out in Greece is an experience filled with hospitality and warmth. When you order food and drinks, it's common to start with a polite "Παρακαλώ" (please) and end with "Ευχαριστώ" (thank you). Tipping is generally appreciated, with 10% being a standard amount. Understanding the menu can enhance your dining experience. Familiarize yourself with standard terms like "ορεκτικά" (appetizers), "κυρίως πιάτο" (main course), and "επιδόρπιο" (dessert). Many menus also feature "ημέρας" (of the day) specials, which are often seasonal and freshly prepared. Don't hesitate to ask the waiter for recommendations; Greek hospitality ensures they'll gladly help.

Dining at a Greek home is a unique experience filled with warmth and generosity. When invited, it's thoughtful to bring a small gift for the host, such as a bottle of wine or a box of sweets. This gesture shows your appreciation and respect. Participating in toasts is another way to engage with your hosts. The phrase "Στην υγειά μας!" (To our health!) is commonly used, and making eye contact while clinking glasses is polite. Meals are often communal, with dishes in the center for everyone to share. This practice fosters a sense of togetherness and hospitality. Expressing appreciation for the meal is essential. Complimenting the host with phrases like "Το φαγητό ήταν υπέροχο!" (The food was wonderful!) is a great way to show your gratitude.

Understanding Greek cuisine and dining etiquette will enrich your experience and help you connect more deeply with the culture. Whether you're enjoying a meal at a local taverna or dining with a Greek family, these insights will guide you in showing respect and appreciation for Greece's rich culinary traditions.

6.5 Greek Mythology and Its Influence on Language

Greek mythology is a fascinating and rich tapestry of stories that have shaped Greek culture and Western civilization. The major gods and goddesses who lived on Mount Olympus are at the heart of these myths. Zeus, the king of the gods, wielded his thunderbolt and ruled the heavens. Athena, the goddess of wisdom, was born fully armored from Zeus's head and became the patroness of Athens. Apollo, the god of light, music, and prophecy, was revered for his beauty and oracle at Delphi. These deities were not just characters in ancient stories; they embodied qualities and ideals that influenced daily life and moral values.

Common myths and stories from Greek mythology include epic tales like the "Odyssey" and the "Iliad." The "Odyssey," attributed to the poet Homer, follows the hero Odysseus on his perilous journey home after the Trojan War. This story is filled with adventures, including encounters with the Cyclops and the enchantress Circe. The "Iliad," also by Homer, focuses on the Trojan War and the hero Achilles. These stories are ancient literature and foundational texts that have been studied and retold for centuries. Their themes of heroism, fate, and the gods' influence on human affairs continue to resonate today.

Greek mythology has left a lasting impact on the modern Greek language, infusing it with expressions and idioms derived from ancient tales. For instance, the term "Achilles' heel" refers to a person's vulnerability and comes from the story of Achilles, whose only weak spot was his heel. Similarly, the phrase "opening Pandora's box" means to unleash unforeseen troubles, originating from the myth of Pandora, who opened a forbidden box and released all the world's evils. These expressions are everyday language, linking modern conversations to ancient stories.

Mythological names are also prevalent in daily life. Greek names, such as Athena and Apollo, are derived directly from mythology. The months of the year and constellations are other areas where mythological references are evident. For example, the constellation Orion is named after a mythical hunter, and the month of January is named after Janus, the Roman god of beginnings, whose concept has roots in Greek mythology. These references are a constant reminder of the enduring legacy of these ancient stories.

The cultural impact of Greek mythology extends beyond language, profoundly influencing art, literature, and architecture. Ancient Greek sculptures often depicted gods and goddesses in idealized human forms, capturing their divine beauty and power. These artistic traditions continued through the Renaissance and into modern times, inspiring countless works of art. Literature, too, is rich with mythological themes. Writers from Shakespeare to James Joyce have drawn on Greek myths to explore complex human emotions and societal issues. Elements like columns and friezes in architecture often feature mythological scenes, blending art and storytelling in public spaces.

Mythological themes continue to permeate modern Greek culture. Festivals, theatrical performances, and even popular media often draw on ancient myths for inspiration. The stories of gods and heroes are retold in new forms, keeping the myths alive and relevant. This continual reinterpretation of mythology reflects its deep roots in Greek identity and its ability to speak to universal human experiences.

Numerous resources are available for those interested in delving deeper into Greek mythology. Recommended books include "Mythology" by Edith Hamilton and "The Greek Myths" by Robert Graves, which provide comprehensive overviews of the myths and their meanings. Websites like theoi.com offer detailed information on gods, goddesses, and mythical creatures. Museums and historical sites, such as the Acropolis Museum in Athens and the ruins of Delphi, offer tangible connections to the ancient world. Visiting these places can provide a deeper appreciation of the myths and their significance in Greek culture.

Understanding Greek mythology and its influence on language and culture enriches your experience and connection to Greece. These ancient stories are not just relics of the past; they are living elements of the present woven into the fabric of daily life. Whether you are exploring the myths for the first time or revisiting them with fresh eyes, the world of Greek mythology offers endless fascination and insight.

6.6 Contemporary Greek Society

The modern Greek lifestyle is a vibrant blend of tradition and contemporary values. Family remains the cornerstone of Greek life, with close-knit family bonds being a defining feature. It's common for multiple generations to live under one roof or nearby, fostering a solid support system. Sundays are often reserved for family gatherings, where extended families come together for a shared meal, reinforcing the importance of familial ties. Social life extends beyond the family, with friends playing a significant role. Greeks enjoy an active social life, frequently meeting friends for coffee or dining out. Work-life balance is highly valued, with leisure activities like evening strolls, known as "volta," and time spent at cafés integral to daily life. These activities provide a space for relaxation and socializing, which is essential for maintaining a balanced lifestyle.

Cultural diversity in Greece has increased significantly due to immigration and the blending of various cultural influences. This multiculturalism is evident in cities like Athens and Thessaloniki, where diverse communities coexist. Immigrants from Albania, Romania, and other countries have brought their customs and traditions, enriching the cultural fabric of Greece. Regional differences also contribute to this diversity. Each Greek region has unique customs, dialects, and culinary traditions. For example, the island of Crete is known for its distinct music and dances, while the Epirus region has unique folk traditions. These regional differences add to the richness of Greek culture, making it a mosaic of various influences and traditions.

Greece faces several current social issues and challenges that impact daily life. The economic situation has been a significant concern, especially following the financial crisis that began in 2009. High unemployment rates and austerity measures have led to economic hardships for many Greeks. Despite these challenges, the resilience and resourcefulness of the Greek people shine through. Environmental concerns are also gaining attention, with sustainability efforts becoming more prominent. Issues like waste management, pollution, and conservation are being addressed through various initiatives to protect the environment. Grassroots movements and local organizations are crucial in these efforts, reflecting a growing awareness and commitment to sustainability.

Pop culture and media in Greece are vibrant and dynamic, reflecting contemporary tastes and trends. Greek music is diverse, with genres ranging from traditional folk music to modern pop and hip-hop. Artists like Sakis Rouvas and Eleonora Zouganeli are well-known figures in the music scene, attracting large audiences with their performances. Greek cinema and television also play a significant role in popular culture. The Greek film industry, despite its size, has produced critically acclaimed films that have garnered international recognition. Television shows, particularly dramas and comedies, are popular among Greeks, offering a glimpse into contemporary Greek life and issues. Digital culture and social media trends are rapidly evolving, with platforms like Instagram, Facebook, and TikTok being widely used. Social media influencers and digital content creators have a substantial following, shaping trends and public opinion.

Understanding contemporary Greek society involves appreciating the blend of tradition and modernity that defines it. The importance of family and social connections, the influence of cultural diversity, the challenges posed by economic and environmental issues, and the dynamic landscape of pop culture and media all contribute to the rich tapestry of Greek life today. These elements collectively shape the experiences and values of the Greek people, offering insight into what makes contemporary Greek society unique and vibrant.

Chapter 7: Interactive Exercises and Practice

This chapter is designed to help you practice Greek engagingly and effectively, allowing you to gain confidence in your language skills.

7.1 Fill-in-the-Blank Grammar Exercises

The verb conjugation is a fundamental aspect of mastering Greek. Let's start with fill-in-the-blank exercises focusing on different tenses to make this process manageable. For the present tense, consider the sentence "Εγώ _____ (διαβάζω) το βιβλίο" which translates to "I read the book." Here, you need to fill in the blank with the correct form of the verb "διαβάζω" (to read). Practicing present tense verbs helps you get comfortable with everyday actions and expressions.

Moving on to the past tense, let's use the sentence "Αυτός _____ (πήγε) στο σχολείο" meaning "He went to school." The verb "πήγε" (went) is the past tense form of "πηγαίνω" (to go). Filling in these blanks will help you talk about past events and experiences. For future tense practice, try "Εμείς _____ (θα δούμε) την ταινία," which means "We will watch the movie." The verb "θα δούμε" (will watch) is the future tense of "βλέπω" (to see). These exercises will prepare you to discuss prospects and aspirations.

Noun cases can be tricky, but fill-in-the-blank exercises can make them easier to grasp. Let's start with the nominative case: "_____ (ο μαθητής) διαβάζει" translates to "The student reads." Here, "ο μαθητής" (the student) is the subject, so it's in the nominative case. For the accusative case, consider the sentence "Βλέπω _____ (την γάτα)" which means "I see the cat." The noun "την γάτα" (the cat) is the direct object, so it's in the accusative case. Moving to the genitive case, try "Το βιβλίο _____ (του παιδιού)" meaning "The child's book." The noun "του παιδιού" (the child's) indicates possession, making it genitive. Practicing these cases will help you form more accurate and meaningful sentences.

Understanding article agreement is crucial for fluid Greek sentences. Try filling in the blanks with the correct definite or indefinite articles. For example, "_____ (ο/η/το) τραπέζι είναι μεγάλο," which means "The table is big." Here, "το" is the correct article because "τραπέζι" (table) is a neuter noun. For indefinite articles, consider "Θέλω _____ (ένας/μία/ένα) καφές" meaning "I want a coffee." The correct article is "ένας" because "καφές" (coffee) is a masculine noun. These exercises will help you understand how articles change to match the gender, number, and case of nouns.

Adjective agreement is another essential aspect of Greek grammar. Let's practice with sentences like "Ο _____ (μεγάλος) σκύλος" which translates to "The big dog." Here, "μεγάλος" (big) must match the masculine noun "σκύλος" (dog). For a feminine noun, consider "Η _____ (όμορφη) γυναίκα" meaning "The beautiful woman." The adjective "όμορφη" (beautiful) matches the feminine noun "γυναίκα" (woman). These exercises will help ensure that your adjectives correctly agree with the nouns they describe, making your sentences more accurate and expressive.

Interactive Exercise: Practice Makes Perfect

Take some time to fill in the blanks of the following sentences. This will help reinforce your understanding and improve your grammar skills.

1. Εγώ _____ (διαβάζω) το βιβλίο. (I read the book.)

2. Αυτός _____ (πήγε) στο σχολείο. (He went to school.)

3. Εμείς _____ (θα δούμε) την ταινία. (We will watch the movie.)

4. _____ (ο μαθητής) διαβάζει. (The student reads.)

5. Βλέπω _____ (την γάτα). (I see the cat.)

6. Το βιβλίο _____ (του παιδιού). (The child's book.)

7. _____ (ο/η/το) τραπέζι είναι μεγάλο. (The table is big.)

8. Θέλω _____ (ένας/μία/ένα) καφές. (I want a coffee.)

9. Ο _____ (μεγάλος) σκύλος. (The big dog.)

10. Η _____ (όμορφη) γυναίκα. (The beautiful woman.)

You'll become more comfortable with Greek grammar by practicing these fill-in-the-blank exercises regularly. This hands-on approach will help you internalize and apply the rules in real-life situations, making your Greek more fluent and natural.

7.2 Vocabulary Matching Games

Learning new vocabulary can be daunting, but turning it into a game makes it more engaging and less intimidating. Picture matching is a fun way to start. Imagine you have a set of cards, each with an everyday object on one side and its Greek name on the other. For example, one card might have a picture of an apple with the word "μήλο" (apple), and another might show a book with "βιβλίο" (book). Flip the cards face down and try to match the picture with the correct word. This method helps cement the connection between the visual image and the Greek term, making it easier to recall the words later. You can do the same with animals like "γάτα" (cat) and "σκύλος" (dog) or food items like "ψωμί" (bread) and "τυρί" (cheese). This exercise is practical and enjoyable, allowing you to learn through play.

Another effective exercise is word-phrase matching. Here, you match Greek words to their English translations or definitions. For example, take the word "καλημέρα" and match it with "good morning," or pair "ευχαριστώ" with "thank you." This helps reinforce your understanding of basic phrases used in daily conversations. Another example could be matching "σπίτι" with "house." Regular practice with these matching exercises can significantly boost your vocabulary retention and make it easier to recall phrases during real-life interactions.

Synonym-antonym matching is another engaging way to expand your vocabulary. You deepen your understanding of word meanings and nuances by pairing Greek words with their synonyms or antonyms. For example, match "μικρός" (small) with its synonym "μικρούλης" (tiny), or pair "μεγάλος" (big) with its antonym "μικρός" (small). These exercises help you learn new words and refine your ability to choose the right word in different contexts. Understanding synonyms and antonyms enables you to express yourself more precisely and adds depth to your language skills.

Contextual matching games take your learning further by placing vocabulary words in sentences that fit contextually. For instance, you might have a sentence like "Πάω στο _____ (σχολείο)" which translates to "I go to school." Here, you need to fill in the blank with "σχολείο" (school). Another example could be "Θέλω να φάω _____ (ψωμί)," meaning "I want to eat bread." Fill in the blank with "ψωμί" (bread). These exercises help you understand how words function within sentences, making using them correctly in conversation easier.

Interactive Element: Vocabulary Matching Game

Create a simple matching game with cards. On one set of cards, write Greek words like "μήλο," "γάτα," and "ψωμί." On another set, draw corresponding pictures or write their English translations. Mix them up, place them face down, and try to find the matching pairs. This exercise can be done solo or with a friend, making it a flexible and fun way to reinforce your vocabulary.

Incorporating these vocabulary-matching games into your practice routine makes learning new words more dynamic and enjoyable. These interactive methods enhance your memory and make the learning process more engaging. As you continue to practice, you'll find that recalling and using new vocabulary becomes second nature, allowing you to communicate more effectively in Greek.

7.3 Dialogue Practice Scenarios

When I started practicing Greek, I realized how crucial it was to get comfortable with everyday conversations. Imagine walking into a bustling Greek restaurant. You're hungry and ready to order. The waiter approaches, and you confidently say, "Θα ήθελα μια σαλάτα, παρακαλώ" (I would like a salad, please). This simple interaction can make you feel more connected and less anxious about speaking Greek. Ordering food is a common scenario; practicing this dialogue can help you correct pronunciation and phrasing.

Another frequent interaction is asking for directions. Picture yourself exploring a new city and needing to find a museum. You stop a passerby and ask, "Πού είναι το μουσείο;" (Where is the museum?). This question is straightforward, but knowing how to ask it correctly can make navigating a foreign city much more accessible. Similarly, shopping at a market requires specific phrases. You might pick up an apple and ask the vendor, "Πόσο κοστίζει αυτό το μήλο;" (How much does this apple cost?). These everyday conversations are practical and essential for daily life in Greece.

Role-playing situations can significantly boost your confidence. Let's say you're checking into a hotel. The receptionist greets you, and you respond with, "Έχω μια κράτηση στο όνομα..." (I have a reservation under the name...). This phrase is vital for smooth check-ins. Or imagine needing a taxi to the airport. You call a taxi service and say, "Χρειάζομαι ένα ταξί για το αεροδρόμιο" (I need a taxi to the airport). Practicing these scenarios helps you prepare for real-life situations, making your travel experiences more enjoyable and less stressful.

Emergencies require specific vocabulary and confidence to handle effectively. Picture yourself feeling unwell and visiting a doctor. You need to describe your symptoms, so you say, "Έχω πόνο στο στομάχι" (I have a stomach ache). Being able to articulate your health issues clearly is crucial. Another scenario could be reporting a lost item. You might say, "Έχασα το πορτοφόλι μου" (I lost my wallet). Practicing these dialogues ensures you're prepared for unexpected situations, giving you peace of mind.

Social interactions are a delightful part of learning a new language. Imagine attending a party and meeting new people. You introduce yourself with, "Με λένε Μαρία, χαίρω πολύ" (My name is Maria, nice to meet you). This simple phrase can open doors to new friendships. Or perhaps you want to invite someone to an event. You might say, "Θέλεις να έρθεις μαζί μας στον κινηματογράφο;" (Do you want to come with us to the cinema?). Practicing these social dialogues helps you feel more comfortable and natural in conversations, making it easier to connect with others.

Engaging in these dialogue practice scenarios regularly can dramatically improve your conversational skills. Each practice session brings you one step closer to fluency, making your interactions in Greek more fluid and enjoyable.

7.4 Self-Assessment Quizzes

When learning a new language, it's crucial to assess your progress regularly. Self-assessment quizzes offer a structured way to test your understanding and identify areas that need improvement. Let's dive into some practical quiz formats to help you evaluate your skills.

Grammar quizzes are an excellent starting point. Multiple-choice questions on verb conjugations can test your grasp of the different tenses. For example, you might see a question like, "Which form of the verb 'to read' fits in the sentence: Εγώ _____ το βιβλίο'?" Your options could be "διαβάζω," "διάβασα," and "θα διαβάσω," testing your knowledge of present, past, and future tenses. Fill-in-the-blank questions on noun cases can deepen your understanding. You might be asked to complete a sentence like, "Ο μαθητής διαβάζει _____ (το βιβλίο)," where you need to choose the correct case. True/false questions on adjective agreement also help solidify your understanding. For instance, "True or False: 'Η μεγάλο γάτα' is correct for 'the big cat.'" These quizzes can pinpoint specific areas where you need more practice.

Vocabulary quizzes are equally important. Matching words to definitions helps reinforce your memory. For example, you might match "καλημέρα" with "good morning" or "ευχαριστώ" with "thank you." Sentence completion with vocabulary words also tests your practical usage. You could be asked to fill in a sentence like, "Θέλω να φάω _____ (ψωμί)," ensuring you know that "ψωμί" means bread. Picture identification quizzes add a visual element to your learning. You might see a picture of an apple and need to choose the correct Greek word from options like "μήλο," "βιβλίο," and "γάτα." These quizzes make vocabulary learning more engaging and effective.

Listening comprehension quizzes are vital for strengthening your auditory skills. Start with questions based on audio clips. You might listen to a short dialogue and answer questions like, "What did the speaker order at the café?" Identifying spoken words and phrases helps you recognize familiar terms in conversation. For example, you could hear, "Πού είναι το μουσείο;" and need to identify the phrase meaning "Where is the museum?" Summarizing spoken dialogues tests your ability to understand and condense information. You might listen to a short story and write a summary in Greek. These activities can significantly boost your listening skills, helping you understand native speakers better.

Cultural knowledge quizzes add depth to your language learning by connecting it to Greek traditions and customs. Questions on Greek customs and traditions can include, "What is the significance of Name Day celebrations?" Identifying cultural symbols helps you understand their importance in daily life. For instance, you might be asked, "What does the evil eye (μάτι) symbolize in Greek culture?" Matching holidays to their descriptions tests your knowledge of significant events. You could see a description like, "This holiday celebrates Greece's independence from Ottoman rule," and you need to match it to "Independence Day (March 25)." These quizzes enrich your understanding of Greek culture, making your language skills more meaningful and contextually relevant.

Visual Element: Sample Quiz Questions

To help you get started, here are some sample quiz questions you can try:

1. Grammar Quiz:

   ○ Multiple Choice: "Which form of the verb 'to read' fits in the sentence: Ἐγώ _____ το βιβλίο'?"

      • A) διαβάζω

      • B) διάβασα

      • C) θα διαβάσω

2. Vocabulary Quiz:

   ○ Matching: Match the Greek word to its English translation.

      • Καλημέρα - good morning

      • ευχαριστώ - thank you

      • σπίτι - house

3. Listening Comprehension Quiz:

○ Audio Clip: Listen to the dialogue and answer, "What
   did the speaker order at the café?"

4. Cultural Knowledge Quiz:

○ True/False: "True or False: The evil eye (μάτι) is a symbol
   of protection against negative energy."

Regularly taking these quizzes, you'll be able to track your progress
and identify areas that need further attention. These assessments reinforce what you've learned and provide a sense of achievement as you
improve.

7.5 Role-Playing Exercises

Role-playing exercises are a fantastic way to practice Greek in
real-world scenarios. They help you build confidence and fluency by
simulating actual conversations. Let's start with structured role-plays.
Imagine visiting a cozy Greek café. You walk up to the counter and
greet the barista with a friendly "Καλημέρα!" (Good morning!). You
then proceed to order your coffee: "Θα ήθελα έναν καφέ, παρακαλώ" (I
would like a coffee, please). The barista might ask, "Με ζάχαρη ή χωρίς;"
(With sugar or without?). You reply, "Με λίγη ζάχαρη, παρακαλώ"
(With a little sugar, please). This interaction helps you practice ordering and familiarizes you with common questions and responses in a
café setting.

Another structured role-play could involve attending a lively Greek
festival. Picture yourself surrounded by colorful stalls and the aroma
of delicious food. You approach a vendor and ask, "Τι συμβαίνει εδώ
σήμερα;" (What's happening here today?). The vendor might explain
the events, and you could follow up with, "Μπορώ να δοκιμάσω τοπικά

φαγητά;" (Can I try some local foods?). This scenario helps you practice asking about events and expressing interest in regional cuisine, enriching your cultural experience.

For improvisational role-plays, consider meeting new neighbors. Imagine introducing yourself: "Γειά σας, είμαι ο/η [Your Name], ο/η νέος/νέα γείτονας/γείτονισσα" (Hello, I'm [Your Name], the new neighbor). You might discuss the neighborhood: "Πώς είναι η περιοχή;" (How is the neighborhood?). This open-ended scenario encourages you to think on your feet and adapt to the flow of conversation. Another improvisational scenario could involve planning a trip with a friend. You discuss destinations: "Πού θέλεις να πάμε διακοπές;" (Where do you want to go on vacation?) and make arrangements: "Πρέπει να κλείσουμε τα εισιτήρια" (We need to book the tickets). These exercises help you practice spontaneous dialogue and decision-making.

Group role-plays add another layer of complexity by involving multiple participants. Imagine hosting a dinner party. You start by inviting guests: "Θα ήθελα να σας προσκαλέσω σε δείπνο στο σπίτι μου" (I would like to invite you to dinner at my house). You then plan the menu: "Τι προτείνετε να μαγειρέψουμε;" (What do you suggest we cook?). This scenario allows you to practice group interactions and collaborative planning. Another group role-play could involve organizing a community event. You assign tasks: "Εσύ μπορείς να αναλάβεις τη μουσική" (You can take care of the music) and discuss logistics: "Πού θα γίνει η εκδήλωση;" (Where will the event take place?). These activities enhance your teamwork and communication skills in Greek.

Feedback and reflection are crucial components of practical role-playing exercises. Peer feedback helps you understand how others perceive your language use and fluency. After a role-play, take a moment to discuss what went well and what could be improved.

For example, a peer might say, "You did great with the greetings, but you could work on your verb conjugations." Self-reflection is equally essential. Think about areas where you felt confident and where you struggled. Setting goals for future role-plays can help you focus your practice. For instance, set a goal to expand your vocabulary for ordering food or to work on your pronunciation during introductions.

Incorporating structured, improvisational, and group role-plays into your practice routine will make your Greek more natural and fluent. Each type of role-play offers unique benefits, from mastering specific phrases to improving spontaneous dialogue. Feedback and reflection ensure that you continue to grow and refine your skills, making each practice session more effective and rewarding.

7.6 Writing Practice: Simple Sentences and Paragraphs

Learning Greek is not just about speaking and listening; writing is equally important. Constructing simple sentences is a great starting point. Begin with subject-verb-object sentences. For example, "Ο Γιάννης τρώει μήλο" translates to "Giannis eats an apple." This basic structure helps you form clear and concise statements. Adding adjectives can enrich your sentences. Consider "Η όμορφη γάτα κοιμάται," which means "The beautiful cat is sleeping." Here, "όμορφη" (beautiful) adds detail to "γάτα" (cat). Practicing these constructions will build your confidence and improve your ability to express yourself in writing.

Once you're comfortable with simple sentences, try writing short paragraphs. Start by describing your daily routine. For instance, "Κάθε πρωί ξυπνάω στις 7 και πηγαίνω στη δουλειά" translates to "Every morning I wake up at seven and go to work." This exercise helps you practice sequencing events and using time-related vocabulary. Another engaging topic is your hobbies and interests. Write about what you enjoy doing in your leisure time. For example, "Μου αρέσει να παίζω κιθάρα τα Σαββατοκύριακα" means "I enjoy playing guitar on weekends." Describing your interests helps you practice new vocabulary and makes your writing more personal and engaging.

Creative writing prompts can take your practice to the next level. Imagine writing an imaginary dialogue. For instance, "Γράψε έναν διάλογο μεταξύ δύο φίλων που συναντιούνται μετά από καιρό" translates to "Write a dialogue between two friends meeting after a long time." This exercise encourages you to think creatively and use conversational phrases. Another fun prompt is writing a short story. Consider "Γράψε μια σύντομη ιστορία για μια περιπέτεια στην παραλία," which means "Write a short story about an adventure at the beach." This allows you to explore narrative structures and descriptive language, making your writing more dynamic.

Peer review is an invaluable part of the writing process. Exchange your written work with a friend or classmate. Provide constructive feedback on each other's writing. For example, suggest ways to improve sentence structure or correct grammatical errors. Reflecting on and revising your writing is also crucial. Look for areas where you can make your sentences more precise or expressive. Setting goals for future writing exercises can help you focus on specific areas for improvement. For instance, you could use more complex sentence structures or incorporate new vocabulary.

Interactive Element: Writing Prompts

Try the following writing prompts to practice your skills:

1. Describe your daily routine in Greek. Include at least five activities you do every day.

2. Write a short paragraph about your favorite hobby. Explain why you enjoy it and how often you do it.

3. Create an imaginary dialogue between two friends who meet after several years. Include greetings, questions about each other's lives, and plans to meet again.

4. Write a short story about a day at the beach. Describe the setting, activities you did, and any exciting events that happened.

By engaging in these writing exercises, you'll find that your Greek writing skills improve steadily. Writing helps reinforce what you've learned in other areas, making your overall language skills more robust. Whether jotting down notes, writing emails, or crafting stories, these exercises make your Greek more fluent and natural.

Chapter 8:
Advanced
Beginner Topics

W hen I first dove into learning Greek, one of the most challenging yet rewarding aspects was mastering verb conjugations in different tenses. This chapter will guide you through the intricacies of the Greek past tense, helping you confidently describe completed actions.

8.1 Past Tense Verb Conjugations

The past tense in Greek, known as the αόριστος (aoristos), is essential for discussing completed actions. Unlike English, Greek differentiates between completed actions and those that were ongoing or chronic in the past. The aoristos specifically denotes actions that have been achieved without focusing on their duration or repetition. For instance, if you want to say, "I wrote a letter," you would use the past tense form of the verb "to write." This tense allows you to convey finished actions, making your storytelling more precise and vivid.

Regular verbs in the past tense follow predictable patterns, making them easier to learn once you understand the rules. Let's start with -ω verbs. Take the verb "γράφω" (to write). In the past tense, it becomes "έγραψα" (I wrote). Here's a simple conjugation table for -ω verbs using "γράφω" as an example:

εγώ έγραψα (I wrote)

εσύ έγραψες (you wrote)

αυτός/αυτή/αυτό έγραψε (he/she/it wrote)

εμείς γράψαμε (we wrote)

εσείς γράψατε (you wrote)

αυτοί/αυτές/αυτά έγραψαν (they wrote)

For -ώ verbs, the pattern is slightly different. Take "αγοράζω" (to buy). In the past tense, it becomes "αγόρασα" (I bought). Here's how it conjugates:

Εγώ αγόρασα (I bought)

εσύ αγόρασες (you bought)

αυτός/αυτή/αυτό αγόρασε (he/she/it bought)

εμείς αγοράσαμε (we bought)

εσείς αγοράσατε (you bought)

αυτοί/αυτές/αυτά αγόρασαν (they bought)

These patterns are consistent across regular verbs, making applying them to new verbs easier as you learn. For example, you might say, "Αγόρασα ένα βιβλίο" (I bought a book) or "Έγραψα μια επιστολή" (I wrote a letter).

Irregular verbs, however, do not follow these patterns and must be memorized individually. Two of the most common irregular verbs are "είμαι" (to be) and "έχω" (to have). In the past tense, "είμαι" becomes "ήμουν" (I was), and "έχω" becomes "είχα" (I had). Here's how they conjugate:

είμαι (to be):

εγώ ήμουν (I was)

εσύ ήσουν (you were)

αυτός/αυτή/αυτό ήταν (he/she/it was)

εμείς ήμασταν (we were)

εσείς ήσασταν (you were)

αυτοί/αυτές/αυτά ήταν (they were)

έχω (to have):

εγώ είχα (I had)

εσύ είχες (you had)

αυτός/αυτή/αυτό είχε (he/she/it had)

εμείς είχαμε (we had)

εσείς είχατε (you had)

αυτοί/αυτές/αυτά είχαν (they had)

Using these irregular forms in sentences helps solidify your understanding. For example, "Ήμουν κουρασμένος χθες" (I was tired yesterday) or "Είχα ένα σκύλο όταν ήμουν παιδί" (I had a dog when I was a child). Practicing these sentences will make these irregular forms feel more natural over time.

Forming negative sentences in the past tense is straightforward. You place "δεν" before the verb. For instance, "I did not go" translates to "Δεν πήγα." This rule applies to both regular and irregular verbs. Here are some examples: "Δεν έγραψα το γράμμα" (I did not write the letter), "Δεν αγόρασα το βιβλίο" (I did not buy the book), and "Δεν ήμουν εκεί" (I was not there). This simple addition of "δεν" changes the sentence's meaning to its negative form, allowing you to express negation clearly and effectively.

Mastering the past tense in Greek involves understanding these patterns and practicing regularly. By doing so, you'll be able to describe past events accurately, whether you're sharing a story or recounting your day. Keep practicing, and soon, these conjugations will become second nature.

8.2 Future Tense Basics

Understanding the future tense in Greek, known as the μέλλοντας (mellontas), is crucial for discussing actions that will happen. The future tense allows you to plan, predict, and express intentions. It's like having a roadmap for your conversations. To form the future tense, you use the particle "θα" followed by the verb in its future form. This tense helps you convey actions that will occur, providing clarity and precision in your speech. For instance, if you want to say, "I will write a letter," you use the future form of "to write," which is "θα γράψω."

The future tense follows consistent patterns for regular verbs that make learning easier. Let's start with -ω verbs. Take the verb "γράφω" (to write). In the future tense, it becomes "θα γράψω" (I will write). Here's a simple conjugation table for -ω verbs using "γράφω" as an example:

εγώ θα γράψω (I will write)

εσύ θα γράψεις (you will write)

αυτός/αυτή/αυτό θα γράψει (he/she/it will write)

εμείς θα γράψουμε (we will write)

εσείς θα γράψετε (you will write)

αυτοί/αυτές/αυτά θα γράψουν (they will write)

For -ώ verbs, the pattern is slightly different. Take "αγοράζω" (to buy). In the future tense, it becomes "θα αγοράσω" (I will buy). Here's how it conjugates:

εγώ θα αγοράσω (I will buy)

εσύ θα αγοράσεις (you will buy)

αυτός/αυτή/αυτό θα αγοράσει (he/she/it will buy)

εμείς θα αγοράσουμε (we will buy)

εσείς θα αγοράσετε (you will buy)

αυτοί/αυτές/αυτά θα αγοράσουν (they will buy)

These patterns are consistent across regular verbs, making applying them to new verbs easier as you learn. For example, you might say, "Θα αγοράσω ένα βιβλίο" (I will buy a book) or "Θα γράψω μια επιστολή" (I will write a letter).

Irregular verbs, however, do not follow these patterns and must be memorized individually. Two of the most common irregular verbs are "είμαι" (to be) and "έχω" (to have). In the future tense, "είμαι" becomes "θα είμαι" (I will be), and "έχω" becomes "θα έχω" (I will have). Here's how they conjugate:

είμαι (to be):

εγώ θα είμαι (I will be)

εσύ θα είσαι (you will be)

αυτός/αυτή/αυτό θα είναι (he/she/it will be)

εμείς θα είμαστε (we will be)

εσείς θα είστε (you will be)

αυτοί/αυτές/αυτά θα είναι (they will be)

έχω (to have):

εγώ θα έχω (I will have)

εσύ θα έχεις (you will have)

αυτός/αυτή/αυτό θα έχει (he/she/it will have)

εμείς θα έχουμε (we will have)

εσείς θα έχετε (you will have)

αυτοί/αυτές/αυτά θα έχουν (they will have)

Using these irregular forms in sentences helps solidify your understanding. For example, "Θα είμαι χαρούμενος αύριο" (I will be happy tomorrow) or "Θα έχω χρόνο το απόγευμα" (I will have time in the afternoon). Practicing these sentences will make these irregular forms feel more natural over time.

Forming negative sentences in the future tense is straightforward. You place "δεν θα" before the verb. For instance, "I will not go" translates to "Δεν θα πάω." This rule applies to both regular and irregular verbs. Here are some examples: "Δεν θα γράψω το γράμμα" (I will not write the letter), "Δεν θα αγοράσω το βιβλίο" (I will not buy the book), and "Δεν θα είμαι εκεί" (I will not be there). This simple addition of "δεν θα" changes the meaning of the sentence to its negative form, allowing you to express negation clearly and effectively.

Understanding the future tense in Greek gives you the tools to discuss your plans, make predictions, and express intentions. By practicing these conjugations regularly, you'll find yourself speaking about the future with confidence and precision.

8.3 Compound Sentences and Conjunctions

One of the most powerful tools in any language is the ability to connect ideas smoothly, creating more complex and meaningful phrases. In Greek, compound sentences allow you to link thoughts and actions, making your speech and writing more fluid. A compound sentence is simply a sentence that joins two or more independent clauses with a conjunction. For example, "Εγώ διαβάζω και εσύ γράφεις" means "I read and you write." Here, two independent actions are connected using the conjunction "και" (and). Conjunctions are crucial in linking these clauses, helping you convey more detailed and nuanced ideas.

Coordinating conjunctions are some of the most commonly used words to connect clauses. They include "και" (and), "αλλά" (but), "ή" (or), and "ούτε" (neither/nor). Each of these words serves a specific purpose in connecting ideas. For instance, "και" (and) is used to add information, as in "Διαβάζω ένα βιβλίο και ακούω μουσική" (I read a book and listen to music). "Αλλά" (but) introduces a contrast, like in "Θέλω να πάω στο πάρκο, αλλά βρέχει" (I want to go to the park, but it is raining). "Ή" (or) offers alternatives, as in "Θέλεις καφέ ή τσάι;" (Do you want coffee or tea?). Finally, "ούτε" (neither/nor) is used for negative statements, such as "Ούτε εγώ ούτε εσύ θα πάμε" (Neither I nor you will go).

Subordinating conjunctions add another layer of complexity by connecting independent and dependent clauses, providing reasons, conditions, or time sequences. Common subordinating conjunctions include "γιατί" (because), "όταν" (when), "αν" (if), and "όπου" (where). These words help you explain the relationship between actions and events. For example, "Δεν πήγα στη δουλειά γιατί ήμουν άρρωστος" (I didn't go to work because I was sick) uses "γιατί" to provide a reason. "Όταν φτάσεις, πάρε με τηλέφωνο" (When you arrive, call me) employs "όταν" to indicate a time sequence. "Αν βρέχει, θα μείνουμε μέσα" (If it rains, we will stay inside) uses "αν" to set a condition. "Όπου κι αν πάω, σε σκέφτομαι" (Wherever I go, I think of you) incorporates "όπου" to describe a location.

Combine simple sentences using coordinating and subordinating conjunctions to practice constructing compound sentences. For example, take the sentences "Εγώ διαβάζω" (I read) and "Εσύ γράφεις" (You write) and combine them using "και" to form "Εγώ διαβάζω και εσύ γράφεις." Next, try fill-in-the-blank exercises with conjunctions. For instance, "Θέλω να ταξιδέψω, _____ δεν έχω χρόνο" (I want to travel, but I don't have time), where you fill in the blank with "αλλά."

Finally, create sentences based on given conjunctions. For example, use "γιατί" to form a sentence like "Δεν πήγα στη δουλειά γιατί ήμουν άρρωστος" (I didn't go to work because I was sick).

Interactive Exercise: Construct Compound Sentences

Combine the following simple sentences using the indicated conjunctions to create compound sentences.

1. "Εγώ μαγειρεύω" (I cook) and "Εσύ καθαρίζεις" (You clean) using "και" (and).

2. "Θέλω να πάω έξω" (I want to go out) but "Βρέχει" (It is raining) using "αλλά" (but).

3. "Θα πάω στην αγορά" (I will go to the market) or "Θα μείνω σπίτι" (I will stay home) using "ή" (or).

4. "Δεν πήγα στη δουλειά" (I didn't go to work) because "Ήμουν άρρωστος" (I was sick) using "γιατί" (because).

By practicing these exercises, you'll become more comfortable using conjunctions to form compound sentences, which will add depth and clarity to Greek communication.

8.4 Introduction to Reflexive Verbs

Understanding reflexive verbs in Greek is another crucial step in becoming more fluent. Reflexive verbs are used when the sentence's subject is also the object of the action. In other words, the subject acts on itself. This concept might sound abstract, but it's pretty straightforward once you get the hang of it. For example, the verb "ντύνομαι" means "I get dressed." Here, the action of dressing is performed by the subject on itself. Reflexive verbs are commonly used in Greek to describe daily routines and personal care actions.

Reflexive pronouns accompany reflexive verbs to indicate that the action is performed on the subject. These pronouns must agree in gender, number, and case with the noun they refer to. The reflexive pronouns in Greek are: μου (myself), σου (yourself), του (himself), της (herself), μας (ourselves), σας (yourselves), and τους (themselves). For example, "Βλέπω τον εαυτό μου" means "I see myself." Here, "μου" is the reflexive pronoun indicating that the action is performed on the subject. Another example is "Εσύ βλέπεις τον εαυτό σου," which translates to "You see yourself." These pronouns clarify the sentence, ensuring the listener understands who is acting.

Conjugating reflexive verbs follows a specific pattern. Let's take the verb "πλένομαι" (to wash oneself) as an example. Here's how it conjugates:

εγώ πλένομαι (I wash myself)

εσύ πλένεσαι (you wash yourself)

αυτός/αυτή/αυτό πλένεται (he/she/it washes himself/herself/itself)

εμείς πλενόμαστε (we wash ourselves)

εσείς πλένεστε (you wash yourselves)

αυτοί/αυτές/αυτά πλένονται (they wash themselves)

Using reflexive verbs in sentences helps solidify your understanding. For example, "Εγώ πλένομαι κάθε πρωί" means "I wash myself every morning." Another example is "Αυτή ντύνεται για το σχολείο" which translates to "She gets dressed for school." Practicing these sentences will help you become more comfortable with reflexive verbs and pronouns, making your Greek more natural and fluent.

To practice reflexive verbs, start with conjugation drills. Take a common reflexive verb like "πλένομαι" and conjugate it with different pronouns. Next, try some sentence completion exercises. For example, fill in the blank in the sentence "Εγώ _____ (ντύνομαι) το πρωί" (I get dressed in the morning). Another exercise could be creating sentences using reflexive verbs. For instance, use "ξυρίζομαι" (I shave) to form a sentence like "Ο πατέρας ξυρίζεται κάθε μέρα" (The father shaves every day).

Consistent practice with reflexive verbs will make them feel more natural in your speech. By using these verbs and pronouns correctly, you can describe personal actions and routines with clarity and accuracy. This will enhance your conversational skills and make your interactions in Greek more engaging and nuanced.

8.5 Indirect and Direct Object Pronouns

When I started learning Greek, understanding object pronouns felt like unlocking a new level of communication. Object pronouns are crucial for making sentences more fluid and concise. In Greek, object pronouns can be direct or indirect, and knowing their differences is essential for clear and accurate expression. Direct object pronouns receive the action of the verb directly, while indirect object pronouns indicate to whom or for whom the action is performed.

Direct object pronouns in Greek replace nouns that directly receive the verb's action. These pronouns include "με" (me), "σε" (you), "τον" (him), "την" (her), "το" (it), "μας" (us), "σας" (you), and "τους" (them). For example, in the sentence "Βλέπω τον Γιώργο" (I see George), "τον Γιώργο" is the direct object. To avoid repetition, you can replace "τον Γιώργο" with the pronoun "τον," making the sentence "Τον βλέπω" (I see him). Another example is "Αγοράζω το βιβλίο" (I buy the book). You can replace "το βιβλίο" with "το," resulting in "Το αγοράζω" (I buy it). These pronouns streamline your sentences and make your speech more efficient.

On the other hand, indirect object pronouns indicate to whom or for whom the action of the verb is performed. These pronouns include "μου" (to me), "σου" (to you), "του" (to him), "της" (to her), "του" (to it), "μας" (to us), "σας" (to you), and "τους" (to them). For instance, in the sentence "Δίνω το βιβλίο στον Γιώργο" (I give the book to George), "στον Γιώργο" is the indirect object. You can replace "στον Γιώργο" with "του," making the sentence "Του δίνω το βιβλίο" (I give him the book). Another example is "Λέω την αλήθεια στην Μαρία" (I tell the truth to Maria). You can replace "στην Μαρία" with "της," resulting in "Της λέω την αλήθεια" (I tell her the truth). These pronouns help clarify to whom the action is directed.

To practice using object pronouns, start with some fill-in-the-blank exercises. For example, "Βλέπω _____ (him)" should be completed with "τον," resulting in "Βλέπω τον." Another exercise could be "Δίνω το δώρο _____ (to her)," which should be completed with "της," making the sentence "Δίνω το δώρο της." Practicing these exercises will help you become more comfortable with object pronouns.

Next, try some sentence transformation exercises where you replace nouns with pronouns. Take the sentence "Αγοράζω το αυτοκίνητο" (I buy the car) and transform it to "Το αγοράζω" (I buy it). Another example is "Γράφω γράμμα στον φίλο μου" (I write a letter to my friend). Transform it to "Του γράφω γράμμα" (I write him a letter). These transformations will help you see how object pronouns can simplify your sentences.

Finally, create sentences using both direct and indirect object pronouns. For instance, take the sentence "Δίνω το βιβλίο στον Γιώργο" and transform it to "Του το δίνω" (I give it to him). Another example is "Λέω την αλήθεια στην Μαρία," which can be transformed to "Της την λέω" (I tell her it). These exercises will solidify your understanding of using both types of object pronouns together, making your Greek more fluent and natural.

Understanding and using direct and indirect object pronouns can significantly enhance your ability to communicate in Greek. By practicing these pronouns regularly, you'll become more adept at incorporating them into your speech, making your sentences more concise and expressive. Keep practicing, and soon, you'll find that using object pronouns becomes second nature.

8.6 Common Idiomatic Expressions

When I first started learning Greek, I quickly realized that understanding idiomatic expressions was crucial to sounding natural and fluent. Idiomatic expressions are phrases whose meanings aren't immediately apparent from the individual words. They add flavor to the language and help you blend in naturally with native speakers. For instance, if you hear someone say, "Βγάζω άκρη," it translates to "I take out an edge," but it means "I figure it out" in English. Knowing these idioms can significantly strengthen your conversational skills and help you understand the nuances of the language.

One of the first idioms I learned was "Κάνω το κορόιδο," which translates to "To play dumb." This phrase is used when someone pretends not to know something. Imagine you're in a social situation where someone is asking difficult questions, and you want to avoid answering. You might say, "Κάνω το κορόιδο," to imply that you're deliberately avoiding the topic. Another common idiom is "Έφαγα τα μούτρα μου," which means "I fell flat on my face." It describes a situation where you've failed or made a significant mistake. For example, if you tried to start a business, but it didn't go well, you could say, "Έφαγα τα μούτρα μου." Lastly, "Είμαι στα μαύρα μου τα χάλια" translates to "I am in a very bad state." It's used to express extreme sadness or distress. If you've had a rough day and everything seems to be going wrong, you might say, "Είμαι στα μαύρα μου τα χάλια."

Understanding the context in which these idioms are used is crucial. For example, you might hear "Κάνω το κορόιδο" in a casual setting among friends who are joking around. Imagine you're at a café, and someone asks you about an embarrassing incident. You could respond with, "Κάνω το κορόιδο," to lighten the mood. In a more serious context, "Έφαγα τα μούτρα μου" might be used in a business meeting to admit to a failure. For instance, you could say, "Στην τελευταία μας προσπάθεια, έφαγα τα μούτρα μου," meaning "In our last attempt, I fell flat on my face." Knowing when and where to use these idioms can make your conversations more engaging and authentic.

To help you practice these idiomatic expressions, try matching them to their meanings. For example, match "Κάνω το κορόιδο" with "To play dumb," "Έφαγα τα μούτρα μου" with "I fell flat on my face," and "Είμαι στα μαύρα μου τα χάλια" with "I am in a very bad state." You can also create sentences using these idioms. For instance, write a sentence like "Όταν με ρώτησαν για το λάθος μου, έκανα το κορόιδο," which means "When they asked me about my mistake, I played dumb." Role-playing scenarios featuring these idioms can also be efficient. Imagine a situation where you must explain a mistake to a friend or a colleague. Use "Έφαγα τα μούτρα μου" to describe what happened. These activities will help you become more comfortable using idiomatic expressions in various contexts, making your Greek more natural and fluent.

Ending the Chapter

In this chapter, you've explored advanced topics like past and future tense conjugations, compound sentences, reflexive verbs, and object pronouns. You've also delved into common idiomatic expressions, learning how they add color and authenticity to your conversations. By incorporating these elements into your daily practice, you'll become more fluent and confident in Greek. As you continue to build on these skills, you'll be well-prepared to tackle even more complex aspects of the language.

Conclusion

As we end this journey, I want to reflect on how far you've come. From the first tentative steps of learning the Greek alphabet to handling complex conversations and understanding the rich cultural tapestry of Greece, your progress is commendable. Remember when you first stared at a Greek street sign and felt lost? Now, you can read it and engage in meaningful conversations with the locals.

Throughout this book, we've explored various topics designed to build a solid foundation in Greek. We started with mastering the Greek alphabet, vowels, and consonants. We moved on to basic grammar, covering everything from subject pronouns to verb conjugations. Along the way, we delved into daily life vocabulary, equipping you with the words and phrases you'll need for dining out, shopping, and navigating the streets of Greece. We didn't stop there; we also tackled more advanced grammar topics and conversational phrases to make your interactions in Greek more natural and fluent.

One of the key takeaways from this book is the importance of consistent practice. Language learning is not a sprint; it's a marathon. By dedicating just 15–20 minutes daily, you've built a habit that will continue to pay off. You've learned to introduce yourself, ask for help, make small talk, and express your preferences and opinions. These skills are not just about words but about connecting with people and understanding a new culture.

Another important takeaway is the role of cultural context in language learning. Understanding Greek customs, traditions, and social norms helps you navigate conversations more effectively. It also enriches your experience, making you not just a speaker of the language but a participant in the culture. These cultural insights are invaluable, whether it's knowing the significance of Greek holidays or understanding dining etiquette.

I want to acknowledge your hard work and dedication. Learning a new language is difficult, but you've shown that it is possible with consistent effort and the right resources. I hope you feel proud of what you've achieved. Remember, every mistake is a learning opportunity and every new word or phrase you master will bring you closer to fluency.

Now, I encourage you to take the next step. Don't stop here. Use the skills you've gained to immerse yourself further in the language. Speak Greek as often as you can, whether it's with native speakers, through language exchange platforms, or even by talking to yourself. Listen to Greek music, watch Greek movies, and read Greek books. The more you expose yourself to the language, the more natural it will become.

Consider joining a Greek language class or finding a language partner to practice with. Travel to Greece if you have the opportunity. There's no better way to learn than by immersing yourself in the environment where the language is spoken. You'll expand your language skills and deepen your appreciation for Greek culture.

As you continue your journey, remember that learning a language is a lifelong process. There will always be new words to learn, new phrases to master, and new cultural nuances to understand. Embrace this journey with curiosity and enthusiasm. Your efforts will open doors to new friendships, experiences, and opportunities.

Finally, I want to leave you with a thought. Learning Greek, or any language, is not just about the mechanics of grammar and vocabulary. It's about connecting with people, seeing the world from a different perspective, and enriching your life. As you continue to learn and grow, keep this in mind. Your journey with the Greek language is just beginning, and the possibilities are endless.

Thank you for allowing me to share this journey with you. I hope this book has been a valuable resource and a source of encouragement. Keep practicing, stay curious, and enjoy every step of your language-learning adventure. Καλή επιτυχία! (Good luck!)

References

1. Wikipedia contributors. (n.d.). *History of the Greek alphabet.* In *Wikipedia, The Free Encyclopedia*. Retrieved September 12, 2024, from https://en.wikipedia.org/wiki/History_of_the_Greek_alphabet

2. GreekPod101. (n.d.). *The only Greek pronunciation guide you'll ever need*. Retrieved September 12, 2024, from https://www.greekpod101.com/greek-pronunciation/

3. GreekPod101. (2022, January 28). *Basic Greek phrases for beginners*. Retrieved September 12, 2024, from https://www.greekpod101.com/blog/2022/01/28/greek-beginner-phrases/

4. GreekPod101. (n.d.). *Counting in Greek: Part I*. Retrieved September 12, 2024, from https://www.greekpod101.com/lesson/basic-bootcamp-4-counting-i

5. Lawless, C. (n.d.). *Subject pronouns - Lawless Greek*. Retrieved September 12, 2024, from https://www.lawlessgreek.com/grammar/subject-pronouns/#:~:text=Greek%20subject%20pronouns%20are%20used,the%20action%20of%20the%20verb

6. TalkPal. (n.d.). *Present tense in Greek grammar.* Retrieved September 12, 2024, from https://talkpal.ai/grammar/present-tense-in-greek-grammar/

7. Do You Speak Greek?. (n.d.). *The indefinite article ένας, μία, ένα / Το αόριστο άρθρο.* Retrieved September 12, 2024, from https://doyouspeakgreek.com/the-indefinite-article-%CE%AD%CE%BD%CE%B1%CF%82-%CE%BC%CE%AF%CE%B1-%CE%AD%CE%BD%CE%B1-%CF%84%CE%BF-%CE%B1%CF%8C%CF%81%CE%B9%CF%83%CF%84%CE%BF-%CE%AC%CF%81%CE%B8%CF%81%CE%BF/

8. Open Book Publishers. (n.d.). *Ancient Greek I - Nouns, pronouns, and their case functions.* Retrieved September 12, 2024, from https://books.openbookpublishers.com/10.11647/obp.0264/ch7.xhtml

9. Olive Tomato. (n.d.). *Greek food dictionary.* Retrieved September 12, 2024, from https://www.olivetomato.com/glossary-of-greek-foods/

10. GreekBoston. (n.d.). *Ordering food in a restaurant in Greece.* Retrieved September 12, 2024, from https://www.greekboston.com/learn-speak/ordering-food/

11. GreekBoston. (n.d.). *Greek shopping vocabulary words to know.* Retrieved September 12, 2024, from https://www.greekboston.com/learn-speak/shopping/

12. GreekPod101. (2020, July 17). *Learn how to ask for and understand directions in Greek.* Retrieved September 12, 2024, from https://www.greekpod101.com/blog/2020/07/17/directions-in-greek/

13. GreekPod101. (2020, December 11). *The most common mistakes in learning Greek.* Retrieved September 12, 2024, from https://www.greekpod101.com/blog/2020/12/11/common-greek-mistakes/

14. Cultural Atlas. (n.d.). *Greek - Etiquette*. Retrieved September 12, 2024, from https://culturalatlas.sbs.com.au/greek-culture/greek-culture-etiquette

15. GreekPod101. (n.d.). *GreekPod101 - Learn Greek with audio & video lessons*. Retrieved September 12, 2024, from https://www.greekpod101.com/

16. Wikipedia contributors. (n.d.). *Help:IPA/Greek*. In *Wikipedia, The Free Encyclopedia*. Retrieved September 12, 2024, from https://en.wikipedia.org/wiki/Help:IPA/Greek

17. GreekBoston. (n.d.). *Learn these Greek tongue twisters*. Retrieved September 12, 2024, from https://www.greekboston.com/learn-speak/tongue-twisters/

18. Greeka. (n.d.). *Culture in Greece & the islands*. Retrieved September 12, 2024, from https://www.greeka.com/greece-culture/

19. Greek Orthodox Archdiocese of America. (n.d.). *Society & culture*. Retrieved September 12, 2024, from https://www.goarch.org/society

20. Greece Travel. (n.d.). *Festivals, celebrations and holidays in Greece*. Retrieved September 12, 2024, from https://www.greecetravel.com/holidays/

21. Etiquette Scholar. (n.d.). *Greece dining etiquette*. Retrieved September 12, 2024, from https://www.etiquettescholar.com/dining_etiquette/table-etiquette/europe-m_table_manners/greek.html

22. TalkPal. (n.d.). *Verb conjugation exercises for Greek grammar*. Retrieved September 12, 2024, from https://talkpal.ai/grammar_exercises/verb-conjugation-exercises-for-greek-grammar/

23. Greek Grammar. (n.d.). *Greek grammar exercises*. Retrieved September 12, 2024, from https://greekgrammar.eu/exercises.php

24. iLearnGreek. (n.d.). *Greek memory games*. Retrieved September 12, 2024, from https://www.ilearngreek.com/Games/MemoryGam e/memorygames.asp

25. Vaia. (n.d.). *Greek dialogue practice: Learning Greek*. Retrieved September 12, 2024, from https://www.vaia.com/en-us/explanation s/greek/greek-rhetoric/greek-dialogue-practice/

26. TalkPal. (n.d.). *Past tense in Greek grammar*. Retrieved September 12, 2024, from https://talkpal.ai/grammar/past-tense-in-greek-g rammar/

27. Alphabetagreek. (n.d.). *How to use the future tenses in Greek*. Retrieved September 12, 2024, from https://www.alphabetagreek.c om/blog/how-to-use-the-future-tenses-in-greek

28. GreekPod101. (2020, January 16). *Greek conjunctions and linking words*. Retrieved September 12, 2024, from https://www.greekp od101.com/blog/2020/01/16/greek-conjunctions/

29. Vaia. (n.d.). *Greek reflexive pronouns: Meaning & examples*. Retrieved September 12, 2024, from https://www.vaia.com/en-us/e xplanations/greek/greek-grammar/greek-reflexive-pronouns/

Made in the USA
Las Vegas, NV
11 December 2024

13869537R00075